The Invisible Assembly Line

Boosting White-Collar Productivity in the New Economy

Daniel Stamp

amacom

American Management Association

New York • Atlanta • Boston • Chicago • Kansas City • San Francisco • Washington, D. C.
Brussels • Mexico City • Tokyo • Toronto

This publication is designed to provide accurate and authoritative information in regard to the subject matter covered. It is sold with the
understanding that the publisher is not engaged in rendering legal,
accounting, or other professional service. If legal advice or other expert assistance is required, the services of a competent professional
person should be sought.

Library of Congress Cataloging-in-Publication Data

Stamp, Daniel
    The invisible assembly line : boosting white-collar productivity
in the new economy / Daniel Stamp.
        p.   cm.
    Includes index.
    ISBN 0-8144-0249-6
    1. White collar workers. 2. Professional employees. 3. Labor
productivity.   I. Title.
HD8039.M39S7 1995
658.3' 14--dc20   95-2437
                                                                      CIP

Printing number

10 9 8 7 6 5 4 3 2 1

Contents

Preface

In August 1799, a band of soldiers with Napoleon's army uncovered an ancient tablet in the town of Rosetta, Egypt. Inscribed on this nearly 2,000-year-old tablet, now known as the Rosetta stone, was a code that had been sought through the millennia—one that would enable anthropologists to decipher the mysteries of hieroglyphics. With this extraordinary discovery, mankind was unable to unlock the secrets of early civilization.

Can a similar code unlock the secrets to business success, for both employees and the companies for which they work? Surprisingly, the answer is yes.

The results of a groundbreaking study, examining the behavior and performance of more than 8,000 men and women active in diverse industries around the world, proves a powerful correlation between a set of identifiable *process skills* and work-related achievement. It indicates that there is a direct relationship between the value a white-collar worker brings to a business and the level of rank and salary the person attains.

The study, conducted by Daniel Stamp, chairman of Priority Management Systems, Inc., and Dr. Peter Honey, Professor of Managerial Learning with the International Management Centres, is based on an innovative measurement tool called the "Process-Skills Analysis" (P-SA). The P-SA is the key to measuring the process-skill proficiency of individuals, teams, and organizations engaged in the increasingly important sector of *knowledge work* (as opposed to physical labor), and for generating dramatic improvements in their effectiveness.

This breakthrough is of particular importance considering the emergence of knowledge work as the key driver for personal, corporate, and even national success in an increasingly competitive global marketplace. The reason is clear: Throughout most of the twentieth century, the world economy has undergone a dramatic shift from the manufacture of product to the formation and delivery of services. In the past decade, this shift has accelerated to the point that today, a mere 20 percent of the global workforce remains in the manufacturing sector; the balance is engaged in knowledge (or white collar) work. In this environment, the conventional manufacturing assembly line is being replaced by its New Economy equivalent: the *invisible assembly line*.

We call it *invisible* because although the connections between people and resources are as important in the knowledge work environment as in the manufacturing plant, this is rarely as apparent. The invisible assembly line concept prompts management and employees to recognize this, to see their place in the scheme of things, and thus to be more productive.

Recognition of the invisible assembly line focuses attention on a critical factor: To thrive in the New Economy, individuals, teams, and organizations must strike a delicate balance between *task* and *process* skills. Task skills are specific to a given job or function, such as a computer programmer's ability to write software. Process skills, on the other hand, are universal to all knowledge workers, enabling them to plan, delegate, and manage the process of work rather than the component tasks.

But an ominous gap threatens progress and productivity in the knowledge worker environment: While the importance of mastering daily tasks has long been recognized, process skills have largely gone ignored. Thus the importance of the P-SA, which measures the strengths and weaknesses of individuals, work teams, and organizations in the eight fundamental process skills, is inherent in productive knowledge work.

The Research Results

Global testing of knowledge workers' process skills reveals a strong correlation between the level of skills and the success achieved by the workers. Key points:

- P-SA scores and salary levels rise in tandem. Workers earning less than $20,000 register a P-SA (or Knowledge Quotient) score averaging 485; workers earning more than $100,000 score an average of 536. (See Figure P-1.)
- Corporate CEOs, government leaders, and the most successful entrepreneurs—men and women at the forefront of the knowledge revoluton—rank at the top of the process-skills proficiency curve. This is further evidence that the eight process skills measured by the P-SA are inexorably linked to individual performance.
- Work with three test groups employed by a Fortune 50 company demonstrates that the same process skills are also closely and directly linked to work-team performance.
- Measurement of eight knowledge work-process skills, coupled with appropriate training designed to emphasize strengths and correct deficiences, dramatically increases P-SA scores and, by extension, individual, team, and organizational effectiveness. (See Figure P-2.)

Figure P-1. Income and knowledge quotient.

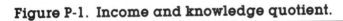
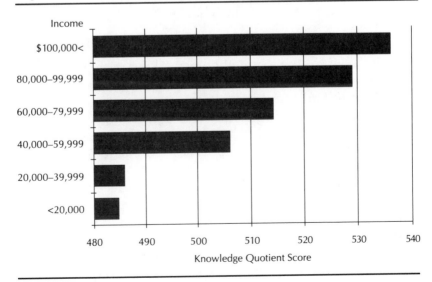

Figure P-2. Average percentage raw gain.

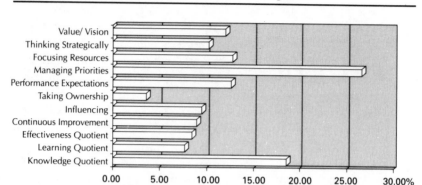

This means the knowledge worker quotient, so critical to success in the New Economy, can be raised to meet the demands of an increasingly competitive marketplace. In effect, individuals and organizations can continuously raise the bar on performance, assuring higher levels of productivity and competitiveness. This is the key to a well-functioning invisible assembly line—and, in turn, to a high level of achievement.

To achieve this result, knowledge workers require the appropriate processes and tools. That's where this book, *The Invisible Assembly Line,* proves invaluable:

- The eight skills described on the following pages are linked into an integrated framework for raising white collar performance. This is the process.
- To help you learn as you navigate through the process, we have included a series of unique forms designed to increase your productivity and raise the levels of group and personal performance. These are the tools.

Taken together, you will learn how to surface your invisible assembly line and, using the proper tools, processes, and skills, how to make the line perform effectively. Viewed in the context of the workplace, this book provides the guidance and resources to help individuals and organizations achieve the higher standards critical for success in the New Economy.

Acknowledgments

This book would not have been written without Mark Stevens, whose encouragement and unwaivering support helped guide me through this project. My debt to Dr. Peter Honey goes further back. His pioneering work in learning technology and behavior provided a starting point for me. He is a friend, a generous supporter, and the very model of a life-long learner.

My thanks also to the generous colleagues who read drafts of this book and improved it with their comments. For their time and guidance, I thank Claire Dillon, Rebekah Whist, and Tee Houston-Aldridge.

The study of over 8,000 men and women was primarily the work of the McGill Management Group. I am indebted to Matthew O'Brien and Elizabeth Stamp for their pioneering work in getting the Process-Skills Analysis project started and, even more so, for finishing it. Brent Krum shuffled bits and bytes to produce software programs of outstanding quality in record time. I thank cover artist, Russ Willms, for his whimsical interpretation of the invisible assembly line.

Finally, there are the men and women of our worldwide franchise network whose boundless energy and enthusiasm make my work possible. To my wife and children—thank you for everything.

The
Invisible
Assembly
Line

1

Leveraging the Legacy of Two Henrys

"Every now and again a door opens and lets the future in."

—British author Graham Greene

Think of the industrial revolution, and legendary figures come to mind: Alexander Graham Bell, Eli Whitney, Thomas Edison, Henry Ford, and Henry Maudslay.

Henry who?

If that's what you're thinking, you're not alone. For some reason (Henry probably didn't have a good PR man), the world has managed to overlook one of the most interesting and important contributions to the ancient quest for ever-greater productivity. Specifically, Henry Maudslay's creation of an industrial assembly line at a Portsmouth, England, naval supply factory in 1803.

The idea was born from a classic imbalance of supply and demand. At the time, the Royal Navy—flexing its might on a global scale—controlled the seas with the firepower of seventy-four gun warships. To fulfill England's territorial ambitions, the pace of shipbuilding had to be accelerated. But a problem emerged: To properly mount its shipboard guns, the navy required 100,000 rigging blocks a year, far outstripping the production capabilities of the Fox & Taylor company, which had the contract to build the blocks and performed all the work by hand.

Sensing opportunity, Frenchman Mark Isambard Brunel, a prominent entrepreneur and engineer, convinced Maudslay—best known as a machine tool inventor—to join him in creating the equipment to produce rigging blocks far faster and less expensively than was possible through Fox & Taylor's manual approach. Maudslay met the test . . . and more. At Brunel's Portsmouth plant, Maudslay created a system that linked the various machines into a coordinated manufacturing process. Fox & Taylor's owner Samuel Taylor was offered the opportunity to join the new venture as a partner and affirmed his faith in manual labor, declaring, "I have no hope of anything better ever being discovered, and I am convinced there cannot be."

Soon after, Fox & Taylor lost its contract with the Royal Navy. It had bowed to the future: The Brunel-Maudslay assembly line, utilizing only ten unskilled workers, was churning out more rigging blocks than Fox & Taylor's shop, which employed 110 skilled craftsmen. The assembly-line plant was so successful that it recovered its investment capital in three years and continued in operation long enough to produce blocks for assault ships participating in the D-Day invasion.

By linking machinery into an integrated production process, Maudslay made a powerful contribution to the industrial revolution and quest for ever-greater productivity. But his more famous successor, Henry Ford, would take the assembly line to a higher plane, using it to support people (rather than to simply eliminate them) and introducing the dynamics of perpual motion.

In creating his line, Ford may have been inspired by an observation of Maudslay disciple James Naysmith: "In all well-conducted concerns, the law of selection of the fittest sooner or later comes into happy action, when a loyal and attached set of men work together for their own advantage as well as that of their employer."

It was at Ford's Highland Park (Michigan) plant that this extraordinary entrepreneur introduced his innovative system for mass production. At the time, some of the most efficient manufacturing processes—in evidence at such producers as the Colt Arms and Singer Sewing Machines plants—consisted of small clusters of workers who produced component parts and then relayed products in process to other teams, who added their own bells and whistles. This represented a significant advance over the traditional manufacturing process, in which craftsmen and laborers functioned independently, but it lacked a key element, *perpetual motion*, that Ford recognized would serve as a catalyst for tremendous strides in productivity.

Building on this epiphany, Ford transformed the sprawling Highland Park factory into a massive conveyor system. All of the elements required to build cars (parts, fasteners, components, chassis) moved to and from his workers automatically, freeing them to focus single-mindedly on the simple assembly-line tasks they were trained to perform. The idea was to maximize the output of people and materials by removing all impediments to productivity. This mission was pursued with abandon.

More than 12,000 employees were linked together in the Ford productivity machine (Henry's *real* invention), and each one was timed, studied, analyzed, and instructed in the quest for greater productivity. Ford and his hand-picked managers were relentless: No sooner were improvements made and recorded than the process would begin anew. At Ford Motor Company, productivity was more than a corporate goal, it was a religion.

This zealous and ingenious engineering of people, machines, time, and motion produced extraordinary results. As demand for the Model T surged, Highland Park employees produced 78,000 cars in the 1911–1912 model year; when production doubled in 1912–1913, so did the workforce. But when production again soared by 100 percent in 1913–1914, Ford's monomaniacal quest for unprecedented productivity demonstrated impressive results: rather than doubling again, the payroll actually dropped by 1,500 workers. The power of the moving assembly line (in full swing that year) enabled Ford to achieve productivity levels that before that place and time would have seemed impossible.

It is safe to say that Henry Ford ushered in the modern workplace. More than any other industrialist, Ford understood the processes of work and how they could be engineered to gain a powerful competitive advantage. His achievement was the creation of an integrated process in which all the components of production—people, machines, raw materials, pulleys, and conveyer belts—were interdependent, producing a synergy that made two plus two equal five. In the process, Ford Motor Company emerged as an industrial behemoth, and the man behind it became the world's richest and most famous capitalist.

Interestingly, Henry Ford's enduring legacy extends well beyond the motor car company he founded. His determination to identify and engineer the processes of work, and to achieve ever-greater levels of productivity, is of great benefit to you and your company in the last decade of the twentieth century and into a new millennium.

How do you benefit from the wizardry of Henry Ford? By looking beyond the systems and procedures that made history at Highland Park and recognizing that every business, whether it produces ceramic coffee cups, electric lawn mowers, legal briefs, or financial statements, has an assembly line, although in most cases it is invisible. What do we mean by *invisible?* That the connections among people, materials, finished products, and time schedules are not apparent. Although this may seem to be a problem, it is really an opportunity in disguise. By learning to identify the components and connections of knowledge work, you can duplicate the synergies Ford used to raise the bar on productivity, competition, success, and profitability.

What's more, you can create a new type of assembly line, driven by a dramatically different catalyst. Just as the mastery of electricity gave rise to the industrial assembly line of Henry Ford, information (represented by the increasing sophistication of computers) can be harnessed to produce today's great strides in productivity.

Interestingly, both technological advances (electricity and computerization) evolved in a similar way. When Edison's miracle was first introduced to the business world, it produced only meager gains in productivity. Steam engines were simply disengaged and replaced by electric versions. Nearly half a century passed before the true power of electricity and electric motors was taken advantage of to produce quantum leaps in manufacturing productivity.

Until recently, computers have failed to achieve their potential, being viewed more as isolated data crunchers than as a powerful technology for restructuring the logistics of business throughout entire organizations. Today, this potential is coming to fruition—and given the headlong move towards the interdependent use of data, reflected by the growth of LANS, HANS, and WANS, groupware, and client-server technology, the assembly lines no longer have to be in one location. They can be spread over towns, regions, nations, and continents.

2

Making Your Assembly Line Visible

"Wise people learn when they can, fools learn when they must."

> —Arthur Wellesley Wellington
> (1769–1852), The Duke of
> Wellington. British General
> and statesman who defeated
> Napolean I at the Battle of
> Waterloo.

If you have difficulty conceiving of an invisible assembly line, that's understandable. In fact, it's a major reason why productivity is stagnant at most companies, especially in white-collar environments where the connections between people, products, material, and time are less evident. The fact is, most people are unable to comprehend what they can't see with the naked eye and touch with their hands. Let's work together to overcome this obstacle by identifying the invisible assembly line in a typical company.

Assume that Status Inc. manufactures high-quality, hand-created wallets made of Italian leather. The business occupies 10,000 square feet of a one-level factory building on Chicago's west side. Two-thirds of the space is devoted to production and inventory, and one-third to administrative functions. This allocation represents more than a division of duties: It is a psychological dividing line between two components of the business, and in the way management views performance and productivity.

What do we mean by this? Let's take a closer look. The production end of the business is structured as a classic assembly line. Long tables, lined on both sides by experienced workers, run the length of the factory. Each laborer has a job: smoothing and cutting leather, stitching and assembling the wallets. Because the line is visible for everyone to see, and because this type of production has always been the subject of productivity campaigns, management has engineered and reengineered the process more than a dozen times, seeking to produce more wallets with fewer workers in less time without jeopardizing quality. Over the years, this effort has borne fruit: By rearranging workers, condensing or automating production steps, and designing easy-to-use tools, the company has increased manufacturing productivity by more than 12 percent. This has enabled Status Inc. to compete more effectively in the upscale wallet market and to gain higher-than-average margins.

But on the other side of the company's building, the space housing the administrative staff, the experience has been dramatically different. Because the company has never thought in terms of boosting white-collar productivity and has no idea of how to do so, employees function on their own, performing what appear to be mostly isolated tasks.

Herein lies the rub. The truth is that like the manufacturing group, the white-collar staff has an assembly line. But because it is invisible, it is poorly structured, often ineffective, and always difficult to reengineer.

For example, the sales department functions primarily by telephone, taking orders from retailers for various style numbers from Status Inc.'s product line. Data on these orders are relayed to manufacturing (which schedules production) and to accounting (which establishes credit and sets up billing). It also interfaces with the customer, hears the complaints, receives new ideas, and the like. If all this white collar knowledge work functioned effectively, production would dovetail with promised delivery dates and customers would be qualified and billed on a timely basis, thus assuring the company of a healthy cash flow. More importantly, customer needs would be relayed to design for future innovation.

But because Status Inc.'s management and employees view the functions of the knowledge worker (as opposed to those of the assembly line workers) as isolated and independent—because they fail to see the invisible assembly line in the company's administrative staff—the work is not performed efficiently. For example, the sales department is chronically late in relaying order information to production, and when it does, it uses a software package that is incompatible with the one in place on the manufacturing end. Similarly, accounting is lackadaisical in checking customers' creditworthiness, and in a high percentage of cases, customer billings are inaccurate. And research and development rarely learns of new, potentially profitable ideas.

All of this blatant inefficiency takes a heavy toll. Because the company has failed to properly engineer the work environment, shipping deadlines are constantly missed (necessitating an unhealthy number of customer refunds), billing is far behind schedule (playing havoc with the company's cash flow), and the company's reputation as a quality vendor suffers across the board. What's more, economies achieved in the manufacturing area are wiped out by losses attributable to the disarray and organizational malaise among the company's knowledge workers. The fact is, regardless of an organization's product or service, the inability to identify the white collar assembly line results in low productivity and, consequently, poor performance.

In today's rapidly changing, highly competitive marketplace, knowledge worker productivity is at a premium. For that reason, you must begin to identify and understand the key components of your invisible assembly line and how they must be integrated to achieve true synergy. In the process, you will want to assess your individual and companywide strengths and weaknesses in each component (making adjustments where necessary) and work to strengthen the connections between the components. This linkage is critically important because the employees and managers involved in an assembly line must develop a high level of interdependency. A sharp focus on the components of the assembly line, and a determination to tighten the links between people, data, products, and time frames, provides management with the discipline and the methodology for building the business. In this context, managers and employees have a framework to guide their efforts and direct their initiatives. As everyone rows in the same direction, individual and corporate productivity soars. That's the power of Henry Ford's genius—updated, reengineered, and applied to you and your company at the threshold of a new millennium.

Big Bang II

Engineering your invisible assembly line is an idea whose time has come. Here's why: In the late 1970s, the world experienced a second Big Bang. It wasn't physical, like the one that occurred at the creation of the universe some 15 billion years ago, but its impact has been every bit as critical. We're talking about the Information Big Bang that is transforming the work we do and the pace at which we must perform.

Big Bang II's impact on change has been more than an incremental acceleration. It has caused discordant, discontinuous—virtually random—change. In this environment, we don't know when change is coming or where it will come from. Our forefathers had half a century (1780–1830) to adapt to the change to an industrial economy, but the accelerated pace of change in the late twentieth century and into the new millennium does not permit a gradual transition.

Paleolithic man hollowed out the first canoe, but 15,000 years passed before Egyptians moved mankind to the next level, building the first ships. In comparison, just eight years (a mere blink of the eye in historical terms) separated the launch of the first man in space and Neil Armstrong's landing on the moon. And today, sophisticated technologies, such as new generations of microchips, are obsolete in a matter of months.

Just as the pace of innovation continues to accelerate, the gap between laboratory innovation and commercial production also has been shortening. If we look back at photography, from the early daguerreotype, it took 112 years (1727–1839) for photography to become a commercial enterprise. In other words, several generations were able to get used to the idea of photography and build it into their social habits before it became available at the general store.

The cycle shortened to fifty-six years from Bell's discovery of the telephone to its emergence as a commercial enterprise. Even as recently as 1922, when television was invented, it took twelve years to get television sets into commercial production. As recently as 1992, IBM's product development cycle times were three years from invention to production. But to keep up with the competition, today's high-tech companies must strive to cut cycle times down to as little as six months.

Our knee-jerk reaction to change in the 1970s through the 1980s was to employ industrial-age economic thinking—streamline the workforce, mechanize work processes (primarily through capital investments in technology), and reduce operating costs by using fewer and less costly employees (often through offshore production). These strategies have effectively increased productivity in the factory, but they have generally failed to generate higher productivity for companies' white collar or knowledge worker components. This cannot be allowed to continue. With information doubling every few years, new tools and new work processes are required to help us develop as effective knowledge workers. By focusing on new approaches, based on engineering the invisible assembly line, we will be able to stimulate white collar productivity, which has been virtually stagnant increasing at the meager rate of 0.2 percent annually (see Figure 2-1).

How do we tackle the challenge of increasing white-collar productivity? To put the issue in context, let's explore an analogy: A frog, like any animal, dropped in boiling water will jump out immediately, desperate to save its life. There is no mystery to this. Leaping from danger—in this case from the threat of destruction—is a basic instinct.

But let's view the response to change from another perspective. The same frog, placed in lukewarm water that is brought to a boil gradually, will adapt to the temperature

Figure 2-1. Disparity between manual- and knowledge-worker productivity.

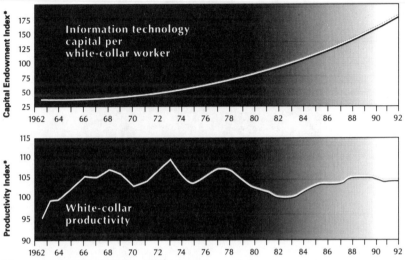

*Measures relative to base performance.

Source: Morgan Stanley estimates based on U.S. Department of Commerce and U.S. Bureau of Labor Statistics data.

Reprinted by permission of *Harvard Business Review*. An exhibit from "Services Under Seige: The Restructuring Imperative" by Stephen S. Roach, September/October 1991. Copyright © 1991 by the President and Fellows of Harvard College; all rights reserved.

change, remaining in the cauldron until it is too late and it is literally boiled alive.

This lesson has extraordinary application in today's workplace. As men and women, corporations and partnerships, organizations and institutions find themselves seeking to cope in an era of unprecedented change, they comfort themselves with the belief that they can *adapt* to change. Like the frog immersed in the ever-warming water, they acclimate themselves to the rising temperatures. Rather than recognizing the danger they face and making a dramatic adjustment to compensate for it, they allow themselves to drift toward a gradual but inescapable demise.

The boiling water is but a metaphor for the real-world change occurring all around us. However, in order to effectively engineer the invisible assembly line and thus improve the pro-

Figure 2-2. Three dimensions of the anatomy at work.

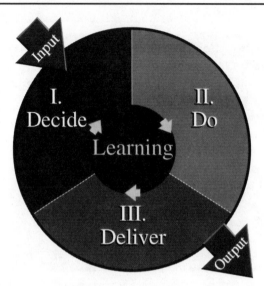

ductivity and effectiveness of knowledge workers, we must first understand the anatomy of work.

All work has three dimensions (see Figure 2-2): deciding, doing, and delivering (the 3 Ds).

1. We must *decide* what we are going to create, make, or process. In other words, our work should begin with the end in mind. To do this, we should ask at the outset, "What are my (our) goals and objectives?" Or, put another way: "What is the purpose of my work?" This helps knowledge workers see beyond short-term tasks, keeping them focused on long-term objectives.
2. Once the "end result" decisions have been made, the work must then get *done:* the formula produced, the product made, or the information processed.
3. After the work is done, it must be *delivered* to an internal or external customer (output).

Note from Figure 2-2 that *learning* is at the core of work. The ability to sharpen skills and acquire new competencies provides all three dimensions of work. Generally, the more people learn about their jobs and the skills necessary to perform them, the better and more productive the work is performed.

Assume Sports Dynamics, Inc., manufactures high-performance tennis rackets. Although the rackets are the by-product of substantial engineering (designed to offer the tennis player the sought-after combination of power and control), the manufacturing process appears straightforward. Management "decides" how to make the rackets, the worker "does" the manufacturing, and the distribution system "delivers" the product. Because we can easily understand the three dimensions of this type of work, and because if it is linear and easily measurable, it is relatively easy to make the process more productive.

The Anatomy of Knowledge Work

Knowledge work (*k*-work) has the same basic anatomy of *deciding, doing, delivering*, but the 3 Ds are more difficult to identify and measure. That's because of the presence of the invisible assembly line. As we have noted, although your company may not produce the physical goods that are often associated with assembly lines, it does process work. Data and raw materials come in one door (input); reports and products go out another (output). It is critical to understand the complex issues at each step of the process in the knowledge work environment.

Deciding

For knowledge workers, a work process is usually initiated by multiple inputs, such as phone calls, e-mail, faxes, or reports, all of which must be interpreted. Without an effective process for interpreting data, individuals are easily overwhelmed. The problem intensifies when we find it necessary to acquire new or different data in order to make a fully informed, effective decision.

Doing

Once a decision has been made, the process of completing the task is also more complicated for knowledge workers. They typically have to *transform* the work, not just add value to it. For example, an idea may be transformed into a memo; an agenda might result from an incoming fax.

Knowledge workers typically find that in order to complete their tasks, they have to interact with other people. But few of them grasp how important the *influencing* phase of work is. Failing to recognize the need for influencing and communicating has been referred to as "white holes"—the space between nodes on an organizational chart into which projects, memos, and reports (the substance of knowledge work) literally disappear. This reflects the fact that all work is part of a system and that work takes place in the context of a process. When things go wrong or work breaks down, it is typically a process (the invisible assembly line) that is out of control, not an individual or team.

Delivery

Not surprisingly, the delivery phase of knowledge work is as complex as the first two phases. It is no longer enough just to finish a report or a project and pass it on. When this Lone Ranger approach is taken, the report or project often disappears into a white hole. To prevent this, knowledge workers must play a *performance* role, making sure that the work they have done is effectively transferred to the appropriate recipient—the customer (whether internal or external).

Let's review this process by interpreting key words for each part of the anatomy of knowledge work:

				Examples
1. *Input*	→			Fax, e-mail
2. *Deciding*	→	Interpret	→	Conflicting data
		→ Acquire	→	Research on-line, interview

Examples

3. *Doing*	→ Transform	→	Write a memo
	→ Influence	→	Hold a meeting
4. *Delivering*	→ Transfer	→	Identify the customer
	→ Perform	→	Make a sales presentation
5. *Output*	→ Multiple types of output	→	Nearly always becomes input for another knowledge worker

Clearly, you must view knowledge work not as a single process but as a series of component parts. This analysis leads to an insight into knowledge work and enables synthesis, which involves combining the components into more efficient processes.

Remember, Henry Ford did not invent the automobile, he brought a scientific discipline to work processes and, as a result, greatly improved productivity in the industrial workplace. By identifying and reconfiguring the invisible assembly line in your business, you can bring similar results to your knowledge work environment.

As we proceed, we will identify precisely what we mean by the *invisible assembly line* and how you can utilize it for yourself and your business.

3

An Eight-Part System for Creating a Productive Force

"Discovery consists of looking at the same thing as everyone else and thinking something different."

—Albert Szent-Gyorgyi

In every company, employees are exhorted, "Use your brains." The implied message: "Do it smarter than you are doing it now." The problem is that few people, or the organizations urging them to perform at a higher level, know how to raise the bar this way. That's where *engineering the invisible assembly line* comes into play, providing a methodology for achieving a higher level of performance. It does so by identifying the eight key components of the line, assessing individual and/or corporate strengths and weaknesses in each, and using a form of engineering to enhance and strengthen the connections between them.

Let's briefly review the eight key components of the invisible assembly line (see Figure 3-1).

Linking Values and Vision

Think of this as road mapping. It refers to the need to align values and vision in order to establish a mission for one's work.

Figure 3-1. Overview of k-Process Typology.

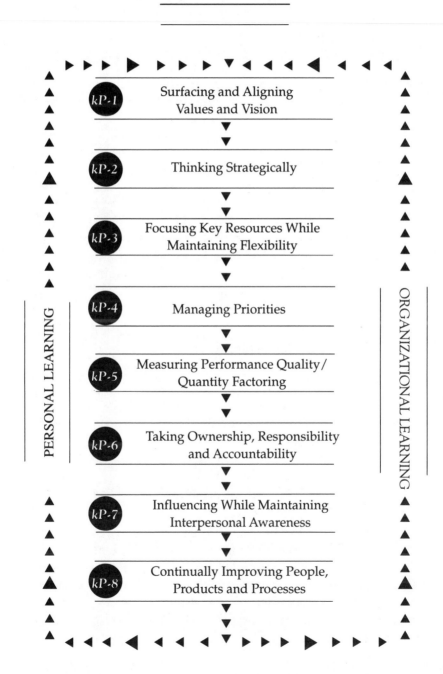

PERSONAL LEARNING

ORGANIZATIONAL LEARNING

kP-1 Surfacing and Aligning Values and Vision

kP-2 Thinking Strategically

kP-3 Focusing Key Resources While Maintaining Flexibility

kP-4 Managing Priorities

kP-5 Measuring Performance Quality/ Quantity Factoring

kP-6 Taking Ownership, Responsibility and Accountability

kP-7 Influencing While Maintaining Interpersonal Awareness

kP-8 Continually Improving People, Products and Processes

This is the first principle for all knowledge workers. It defines the purpose of work and answers the question, "Why are we doing this?" This focus on objectives ensures that all tasks and activities, whether planned from the start or added in midstream, are consistent with the ultimate goal.

As we have noted, this is the most vital part of knowledge work: Always start with the end in mind. Had IBM heeded this rule, it would have avoided its sideways drift from a customer focus to a blind mainframe allegiance.

Skills Required

1. *Conceptual thinking.* Identifying key issues, seeing relationships, and drawing elements together into broad, coherent frameworks.
2. *Strategic thinking.* Taking the longer term into consideration and developing broad-scale objectives.
3. *Innovation.* Generating original and imaginative ideas and solutions to problems.

Warning signs of a poor personal/corporate rating in the ability to surface and align values and vision are:

1. Low motivation
2. Lack of effectiveness
3. Poor morale and lack of trust

Thinking Strategically

Think of this as seeing both the forest and the trees. Thinking strategically determines the *what* of our work. Ideally, it leads to a mission—a clearly defined statement of goals. The mission gives congruence to our values and vision. Once the exclusive domain of top management, today strategic thinking must be pervasive (practiced individually and collectively) throughout the company.

Skills Required

1. *Conceptual thinking.*
2. *Results orientation.* Focusing attention on key objectives.
3. *Information seeking.* Gathering information from key sources to assist in problem solving.

Warning signs of poor strategic thinking are:

1. An ongoing crisis environment
2. Confusion
3. Ambiguity

Focusing Key Resources While Staying Flexible

The idea is to focus key resources—personnel, equipment, time, capital, and technology—on accomplishing stated strategies while maintaining flexibility so that the company and its employees can quickly and effectively adapt to change.

This process asks what resources (people, time, equipment, money, technology) are required to achieve the mission. It ensures that resources are deployed effectively, which is fundamental to achieving maximum productivity. The paradox of this process is that continuously asking questions ("What resources are needed for a given situation?") helps you to profit from change by seizing upon unexpected opportunities.

A continuous process of reviewing resource allocation ensures both focus and flexibility.

Skills Required

1. *Analytical thinking.* Carrying out diagnoses, logically breaking down problems into their essential elements, and developing solutions.
2. *Adaptability.* Maintaining effectiveness in different situations, environments, and cultures.
3. *Flexibility.* Altering behavior and opinions in the light of new information on changing situations.

Warning signs of poorly focused resources are:

1. Poor ability to cope with change
2. Inability to delegate

Managing Priorities

This is done to keep the tail from wagging the dog. Unless priorities are established and carefully managed, work will drift rather than drive toward achieving stated objectives. Managing priorities helps everyone, and the company, accomplish their missions. Here's the key point: From managing priorities springs the ability to get the right job done, not just the job done right. This is a critical distinction, and a building block of effectiveness.

Skills Required

1. *Strategic thinking.* Focusing on the important, not just the urgent.
2. *Results orientation.* Seeking effective outcome.
3. *Self-control.* Continuing to perform effectively in stressful and difficult circumstances.

Warning signs of poor priority management are:

1. Lack of focus
2. Ineffectiveness
3. Lack of understanding of the company's vision

Defining Performance Expectations (Q² Factoring) Factoring—Balancing Quality and Quantity

This defines performance and makes it possible to measure improvement.

Think of this as the control process of the invisible assembly line, keeping in mind that knowledge worker productivity is defined and measured as a combination of quality and quantity.

Every knowledge worker needs to define how much (quantity) work must be produced and how good (quality) it must be. This is done, in part, by measuring the quantity/quality balance on every project, as ascertained by both the doer and the recipient of the work, and making adjustments where necessary.

Skills Required

1. *A focus on efficiency.* Looking for the best uses of resources.
2. *Concern for achieving standards.* Pursuing excellence in line with organizational benchmarks and values.
3. *Thoroughness.* Seeking completeness and accuracy.

Warning signs of a lack of balance between quantity and quality are:

1. High stress
2. Poor quality

Taking Ownership, Responsibility, and Accountability

Think of this as power to the people. As the company vests employees with ownership, responsibility, and accountability for their jobs, they measure their own progress and take proactive steps to boost performance, further increasing productivity. So viewed intelligently, power to the people is actually power to the company.

The goal of this process is to build responsibility for productivity and performance into every knowledge worker's job, regardless of the level of difficulty or skill. To accomplish this, supervisors must form partnerships with the people who are doing, authorizing the doers to take ownership of their jobs.

Ownership leads to both personal and team accountability, which, in turn, leads to higher levels of self-imposed responsibility. Put simply, people work harder to get the job done right.

Looking back to the first component of the integrated work process, linking values and vision, it is important to understand that the beginning and end of superior performance is the doer's knowledge of the job. This demonstrates the importance of viewing all eight assembly line components as part of a holistic process.

Skills Required

1. *Positive self-image.* Believing in oneself.
2. *Initiative.* Engaging in proactive behavior; seizing opportunities.
3. *Concern for impact.* Actively anticipating and responding to the feelings, needs, and concerns of others.

Warning signs of a lack of ownership, responsibility, and accountability are:

1. Failure to take personal responsibility
2. Weak leadership
3. Finger pointing (as opposed to cooperation and collaboration)

Influencing While Maintaining Interpersonal Awareness

This focuses on the power of persuasion, and requires a high level of competence in communications and negotiating.

Why is the power of persuasion so important? As companies adopt flatter management structures, replacing hierarchical reporting relationships with personal empowerment, missions must be clearly defined and communicated to everyone. Why? Because if knowledge workers are to perform productively, they must achieve a high level of *interdependence*, working in teams rather than as islands unto themselves. And as team members, they must be capable of influencing the behavior and attitude of others. This is an essential distinction between people who are functioning independently and those who are part of an assembly line and cognizant of their role on it.

Skills Required

1. *Strategic influencing.* Being aware of different forms and sources of influencing in choosing between different influencing strategies.
2. *Interpersonal awareness.* Drawing inferences about and maintaining awareness of others' interests, moods, and concerns.
3. *Rational persuasion.* Building persuasive arguments based on logic, data, and the objective merits of the situation.

Warning signs of a lack of interpersonal awareness are:

1. Turf protection
2. Communications barriers
3. "Not-invented-here" syndrome

Continually Improving People, Products, and Processes

In this era of constant change, the customer demands ever-higher standards of quality, variety, customization, convenience, and timeliness. To thrive—in fact, just to survive—we must continually challenge the status quo, and make the goal of *improvement through learning* a key part of every knowledge worker's job.

The measurement of ability and willingness to learn, both as an individual and as an organization, is critical to achieving success. Thus, engineering your invisible assembly line is vitally important. Because this provides an x-ray for identifying the key characteristics of your business and a step-by-step system for integrating (and thus unleashing the power of) the major work process components, it guides companies and individuals to a new level of achievement and productivity. As such, it is an essential tool for every company and every individual seeking self-improvement.

Required Skills

1. *Ability to learn.* Quickly understanding and applying information, concepts, and strategies.
2. *Self-development orientation.* Taking continuous action to improve personal capability.
3. *Development orientation.* Identifying and providing opportunities to improve the capabilities of other people.

Warning Signs of a lack of learning and continuous improvement are:

1. Inability to change
2. Fear and mistrust
3. Complacency

Daniel Boorstein once said, "The greatest obstacle to discovery is not ignorance—it is the illusion of knowledge." In other words, you may think you have the knowledge skills to succeed in today's markets, but that assumption may well be based on skills developed (and considered appropriate) for another time in history. Engineering the invisible assembly line will ensure that you and your company gain the skills and methodologies to win now—and in the future.

4

Linking Values and Vision

"Wisdom is the supreme part of happiness."

—Sophocles, *Antigone* (440 B.C.)

Linking values and vision is the key prerequisite for productive knowledge work. As we have noted before (but it bears repeating), high-performance knowledge work must start with the end in mind. That's because the planned and desired output should determine what work should be done.

If we accept the fact that we have to see the end before we start, then we should recognize that a personal vision is pivotal to an intelligent and motivated workforce. Without a personal vision, our life and our work can easily become a series of meaningless inputs without purpose, pride, or ownership—just work! No wonder Henry David Thoreau said that "most people lead lives of quiet desperation."

Clearly, we cannot function as empowered or motivated workers if we are being "sold" someone else's vision. The only vision that motivates us is our own.

This raises a critical question: How do we go about identifying and surfacing a personal vision? The answer lies in the discovery that personal vision is rooted in the individual's values, dreams, and aspirations. By exploring this virtually unchartered territory, we can discover and create a personal vision.

To begin, let's identify just what we mean by values, and why they are important to us.

Values share these common characteristics:

- You choose them.
- You know and accept the consequences of living with them.
- You prize and cherish them.
- You publicly proclaim them.
- You act on them.
- You act on them repeatedly.

It is important to understand that values ultimately trigger all of our actions, both positive and negative. Since values are this important, we should pay close attention to them. We can create a strong personal vision only if we first gain a comprehensive understanding of our personal values.

Let's turn the spotlight on you by investigating your personal values.

EXERCISE

A. Write down six values that are important to you.

1. _____
2. _____
3. _____
4. _____
5. _____
6. _____

B. Consider each of these values. Select the one that is least important to you and cross it out. Do the same for the next three least important values.

C. Now you are down to two values. Sorry, but yes, we are going to ask you to discard one of them. This is the "lifeboat test"—one life jacket and two precious values—and one has to go! It may be difficult, but choose the less important of these remaining values and cross it out.

D. You now have one key value left on the page. Write it down:

_____

How much time have you given this value this month/ week?

_____

If the answer is "very little," perhaps you should cross this one out too. You need clearly identified, deeply held values in order to better manage your allocation of your time, your job, your company, and your career.

There are two messages for you. First, we often fail to allocate sufficient time to our most precious and closely held values. Second, your values provide the parameters for your vision. This means that values and visions are inextricably connected. Without values, your vision will be blurred, and without vision, your values will not be given life and full expression.

Values Gap

If our lives and work are to have real purpose, then it is paramount that we surface our values and give them meaning by writing them down. But be aware: Turning values into written statements often reveals a "values gap" between what you are doing and what you deem to be truly important. This may sound ominous, but it is actually an opportunity in disguise. That's because the values gap (often evidenced by personal dissatisfaction) can be turned into your most potent self-development tool. For this breakthrough to occur, you must allow the gap to serve as *tension for change*. This is the difference between where you are (current reality) and where you would like to be (values/vision). The greater the gap or difference, the higher your tension for change, or Tension Quotient:

$$Va\text{(Values)} + Vi\text{(Vision)} - CR \text{ (Current Reality)} = TFC \text{ (Tension for Change)}$$

As you perform the following exercise, you will assess for yourself the areas of your performance in which you have a tension for change.

We will explore six key-value areas that influence both your personal and organizational life.

INSTRUCTIONS

To discover how to establish your Tension Quotient (TFC Rating), use the TFC charts (Figures 4-1 and 4-2) and follow these six steps:

Step 1   For each area, write a brief value statement in the first column (see the example on the TFC charts). There are six areas on each chart, for each major value area on the values wheel.

Step 2   In the second column, write a brief statement of the future that shows you clearly living up to the stated value.

Step 3   Write a brief description of your current reality in the third column. Be honest, but don't sell yourself too short!

Step 4   In column 4, rate your current reality performance on a scale of 1 to 10, where 10 is a perfect match between the vision and your current reality and 0 indicates a mismatch (meaning that your vision and your current reality are dramatically different).

Step 5   Subtract your current reality rating from the perfect 10 to discover your Tension Quotient.

Step 6   Transfer your scores onto the tension quotient summary (Figure 4-3).

(text continues on page 33)

Figure 4-1. Tension for change application exercise—personal values.

TENSION FOR CHANGE
APPLICATION EXERCISE

PERSONAL VALUES

	Column 1	Column 2	Column 3	Column 4	Column 5	Column 6
	Value	Vision	My Current Reality	CR Rating (0 to 10)	Tension Quotient (10-CR)	Weekly Development Strategy
Example	It is important to me... ...to be physically fit.	I consistently participate in physical activities on my own and with family and friends.	I get breathless walking to the bus stop.	2	8 (10 - 2)	Week 12
Work	It is important to me...					
Learning	It is important to me...					

(continues)

Figure 4-1 (Continued.)

	Column 1	Column 2	Column 3	Column 4	Column 5	Column 6
	Value	Vision	My Current Reality	CR Rating (0 to 10)	Tension Quotient (10-CR)	Weekly Development Strategy
Physical	It is important to me…					
Social	It is important to me…					
Family	It is important to me…					
Spiritual	It is important to me…					

Figure 4-2. Tension for change application exercise—organizational values.

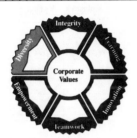

ORGANIZATIONAL VALUES

	Value	Vision	My Current Reality	CR Rating (0 to 10)	Tension Quotient (10-CR)	Weekly Development Strategy
	Column 1	Column 2	Column 3	Column 4	Column 5	Column 6
Example	*It is important to me...*					
Example	*...to respect all people, regardless of age, sex, culture, etc.,.*	*I will behave towards people from other cultures or minorities with open-minded curiosity and learn from our differences.*	*I tend to judge people with certain prejudice and this affects my behavior towards them.*	*5.5*	*4.5 (10 - 5.5)*	*Week 3*
Integrity	*It is important to me...*					
Integrity						
Integrity						
Learning	*It is important to me...*					
Learning						
Learning						

(continues)

Figure 4-2   (Continued.)

	Column 1	Column 2	Column 3	Column 4	Column 5	Column 6
	Value	Vision	My Current Reality	CR Rating (0 to 10)	Tension Quotient (10-CR)	Weekly Development Strategy
Innovation	It is important to me…					
Empowerment	It is important to me…					
Teamwork	It is important to me…					
Diversity	It is important to me…					

Figure 4-3. Tension quotient summary.

INSTRUCTIONS:

1. Transfer your CR scores for each area (*from column 4*) and plot them on the graph below.
2. The *TQ* is the gap between your CR mark and 10 (the vision).

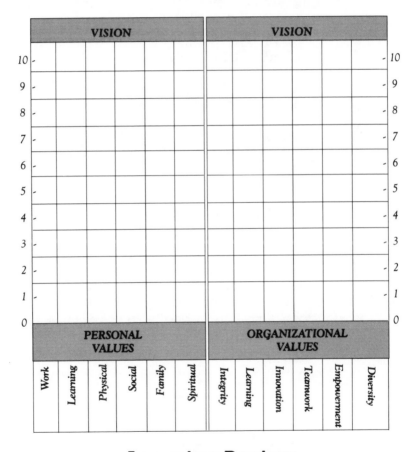

Learning Review

Read through the learning review below and check those items that have particular relevance for you. Once you have completed this, circle the *one item* that you feel has been a learning breakthrough and discuss its significance with a coworker or friend.

☐ The definition and understanding of a value
☐ The way values underpin your personal vision
☐ There is often a gap between your values and vision and your current reality
☐ $Va + Vi - CR = TFC$ (a tension for change formula)
☐ The application exercise has provided you with a tool for discovering your greatest TFCs (tensions for change).

Closing the Values Gap

Happiness and motivation come to us most often as the by-products of pursuing meaningful goals and visions.

—*D. Stamp*

LEARNING TRANSFER

Keep in mind that our goal is to raise the bar on productivity, individually as well as collectively. Before moving on in this book, you should begin work on your personal plan by identifying your strengths and weaknesses. Write a brief statement encapsulating your strengths and weaknesses as identified during your work in this chapter.

_____

_____

_____

_____

_____

_____

_____

_____

5

Thinking Strategically

"The best way to predict the future is to invent it yourself."

—John Sculley, former CEO of Apple Computer

As we have already learned, *values* are at the core of where we want to go and what we want to become. *Vision* is a statement of these values.

Combined, these elements define the purpose of our work—we must find a way to express and implement them on a day-to-day basis. Simply put, we are referring to the ability to think strategically—not for the sake of creating ivory-tower strategies (in the form of dust-collecting reports), but instead with the aim of producing practical strategy that guides the work of the assembly-line participants, individually and collectively. This powerful synergy is achieved when values, vision, and implementation are linked.

A powerful process called *mind-mapping* can help you achieve this linkage, and thus think strategically. It provides a framework for integrating values, visions, and implementation, as well as a means of measuring performance. What's more, the mind-mapping process encourages you to think creatively—to make statements about your goals, visions, and mission, and connect them in a way that generates new ideas.

Strategic Statements

Strategic statements, which lend themselves the mind-mapping process, are precise declarations of what you want to achieve. One of the most famous strategic statements was made at the outset of the 1960s when President John Kennedy declared, "By the end of this decade, we shall put a man on the moon and return him safely to earth." (You can use this as a model for making your own strategic statements, albeit on a smaller scale!)

When writing these statements, keep in mind that they should be *S.M.A.R.T.*:

Specific: To identify what should be accomplished and by when.

Measurable: Providing a basis for measuring results.

Attainable: Is the goal reasonable/achievable within the time constraints?

Relevant: Is it worth pursing; important?

Trackable: Will you be able to track the progress?

In Figure 5-1, you will find a personal and organizational strategic statement form for your use. Each statement should be written with the end in mind and should also include indicators of success. A S.M.A.R.T. checklist will keep your statements from becoming too fuzzy. Remember, the goal is to pinpoint what you want to achieve, so that all of the people involved in the assembly line do more than work—they integrate their activities to achieve collective goals.

Personal Mission Statement

Mind-mapping can help you prepare a *personal mission statement*. This exercise is best completed at home, preferably on a weekend, when you feel relaxed and energized.

Your mission statement will focus on these key elements:

- Your *guiding principles*
- What you want to *be* (character)
- What you want to *do* (achievement and contributions)

Figure 5-1. Strategic statements form.

Area:	
Value:	*End Result:*
Vision:	*Indicators of Success:*
	Specific ☐ Measurable ☐ Attainable ☐ Relevant ☐ Trackable ☐

Area:	
Value:	*End Result:*
Vision:	*Indicators of Success:*
	Specific ☐ Measurable ☐ Attainable ☐ Relevant ☐ Trackable ☐

Area:	
Value:	*End Result:*
Vision:	*Indicators of Success:*
	Specific ☐ Measurable ☐ Attainable ☐ Relevant ☐ Trackable ☐

What Are My Guiding Principles?

The dictionary defines "principle" as a fundamental truth or law that is the basis for reasoning or action. It is also defined as a personal code of conduct. The closer our strategic and value statements come to our guiding principles, the more valuable and useful they become.

As you move through this process of self-evaluation, you will have to answer two key questions: What do I want to be? What do I want to do?

What Do I Want to Be?

This question explores the character strengths and qualities that you want to develop. You are really asking, "For what do I want to be known in life?"

Sample Statement of "What I Want to Be" (See Figure 5-2)

• I will strive for win-win outcomes and will neither take flight nor fight if faced with conflict.

Figure 5-2. Mind map—what do I want to be?

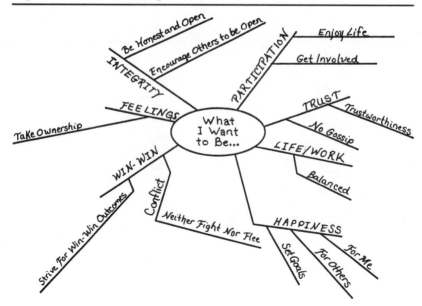

- I want to conduct my business and personal life with integrity, be honest and open, and encourage others to be this way. I will be known for my trustworthiness.

Think about how *you* would answer "What I Want to Be," and make notes on this. You will use the information in drafting your personal mission statement.

What Do I Want to Do?

This question explores prospective achievements—that is, what you want to contribute and accomplish.

Sample Statement of "What I Want to Do" (See Figure 5-3)

- At work, I would like to lead project teams and acquire team leadership skills.
- At home, I would like to plan a five-year mortgage paydown.

Figure 5-3. Mind map—what do I want to do?

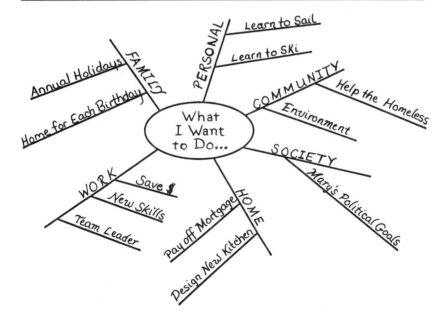

Spend more time considering your answer to "What I Want to Do," and prepare a draft of some of the key elements for your mission statement.

Drafting the Personal Mission Statement

Now that you have identified what you want to be and what you want to do (based, in part, on your underpinning philosophies), it is time to draft your personal mission statement. Use this page for the draft, recognizing that it is likely to change over time. (Because of this, use a pencil.) If you need inspiration, consider the sample personal mission statement shown in Figure 5-4.

Figure 5-4. Sample personal mission statement.

<u>*Family*</u>
My first loyalty is to the relationship between Sandy and myself. It is important for me to love and honor Sandy, as I would have her love and honor me.

My second loyalty is to my children. It is important to me:
- *to be a positive role model for them.*
- *to help them to define and achieve their personal goals.*

<u>*Interdependent Relationships*</u>
I value interdependent relationships with family, colleagues, and friends. It is important to me:
- *that my behavior, language, and actions reflect my principles and values.*
- *that my spiritual, career, personal, and family activities receive equal priority.*
- *to share my life with people who are honest, positive, and enthusiastic. I respect those who take responsibility for their actions and who fulfill their commitments.*

<u>*Security*</u>
I value financial security for my immediate family. It is important to me:
- *that I do work that is meaningful and consistent with my principles and values.*
- *that I seek opportunities for creating shared wealth.*
- *to take reasoned risks in order to achieve financial goals.*

<u>*Learning, Creativity, and Fun*</u>
I value any and all opportunities for learning, innovation, and fun. It is important to me:
- *to ensure that the people I meet feel able to share their feelings, free from fear of judgment.*
- *to focus on the quality of input, secure in the knowledge that quality input and effort will generally result in the desired outcome.*

<u>*Physical Well-Being*</u>
I value living and working in ways that contribute positively to my health and environment. It is important to me:
- *that I ensure my physical well-being through regular exercise.*
- *that I contribute to the preservation and regeneration of my social and natural environment.*

Bob Johnson	*7th July*
Signed	Date

Real World Close-Up

After spending ten years with a global consulting firm, Franklin H. achieved what his peers viewed as a crowning achievement—the high point of a career: He was elected a partner.

Although Franklin was pleased with his achievement, from his perspective, this was only a stepping stone. He was determined to rise from the ranks of more than 500 partners, driving the firm to greater success and, in the process, enhancing his own position of leadership. He would pursue his goal by creating a personal mission statement designed to address the two key components:

1. What do I want to be?
2. What do I want to do?

As he crafted his statement, Franklin answered the questions this way:

What do I want to be?
In a firm of technical specialists in finance, human resources, and marketing, I will be different, focusing on the firm's internal issues. As the partners struggle with ways and means of building the practice, I will emerge as the in-house organizational expert—the point person for tying together the components of the invisible assembly line and, as a result, achieving the highest levels of synergy and productivity.

What do I want to do?
I will become a member of the firm's executive committee, and, in turn, its managing partner. Guided by my personal mission statement, and the underlying strategy it represents, I will embark on a course that offers a clear path to the top.

Learning Review

Read through the learning review below and check those items that have particular relevance for you and/or your team. Once you have completed this, circle the *one item* that you feel has been a learning breakthrough and discuss its significance with your co-workers.

☐ Your mission is the purpose of your work on a day-to-day basis.
☐ Strategic statements develop out of your values and vision.
☐ Strategic statements, like goals, have to be *S.M.A.R.T.*
☐ A *personal mission statement* is a vital tool for navigating along the invisible assembly line because it gives meaning and substance to your work. It takes time to develop, but it can lead to transformational change in your career and/or your company.

LEARNING TRANSFER

Write a brief statement encapsulating your strengths and weaknesses as identified during your work in this chapter.

_____

_____

_____

_____

_____

_____

_____

_____

6

The Delicate Balance: Focusing Key Resources While Maintaining Flexibility

"By the work, one knows the workman."

—Jean de la Fontaine, *Fables* (1668)

Before we proceed, let's take a step backwards, putting your perception of the assembly line in context. Before you opened this book, you thought of the assembly line as a means of producing physical goods. However, as we have discovered, another assembly line, albeit an invisible one, is equally prevalent (and important) in the workplace. Because this concept is still new to you, it may be hard to visualize. To help bring it to life, let's explore another example of the invisible assembly line and how it can be engineered to achieve maximum productivity.

Imagine taking a seat inside the century-old law firm of Smythe, Smythe, & Smythe. As far as the partners of this venerable legal institution are concerned, the last thing you will find within their hallowed halls is an assembly line. From their perspective, low-wage auto workers and PC assemblers make their living on assembly lines, but distinguished men and women from Yale, Harvard, and Oxford—no way. They may share a firm name, use a common library, and collaborate on scholary issues, but that, they will proclaim with pride, is the extent of their interdependence.

As much as Smythe's partners prefer to think of themselves as engaging in purely intellectual pursuits—spending their days in the office thinking and pontificating—the unvarnished truth is that they participate in the planning, production, and distribution of an intangible *product*: legal representation. Although they refuse to recognize or admit it, their law firm is more like a white-collar factory producing a knowledge-based product than like a haven for scholarly thought. Within their "hallowed halls," major elements of an assembly line are in place—it's just that no one chooses to see it that way. It remains invisible.

But if we peer through the camouflage, look what we see:

- Client requests for legal services, known in the production environment as work orders, come in over the transom.
- Raw materials are delivered in the form of physical evidence, discovery, legal research, and investigations.
- Schedules are established to meet contractual deadlines and court calendars.
- Responsibilities are assigned by the managing partner, who assembles teams of partners, associates, and paralegals to service the cases.
- Accounts payable bills the clients.
- Accounting collects receivables and deposits them in the firm's bank accounts.
- Administration monitors billable hours, establishing partners' earnings and client fees.
- Once cases are successfully completed, Smythe's marketing director distributes press releases designed to generate positive publicity for the firm's performance, with the goal of generating additional business down the road.

Clearly, Smythe, Smythe, & Smythe is home to an interdependent group of people, responsibilities, and projects—an

assembly line. Why is this important? Because only by identifying the line and its component parts can management engage
in the engineering process that can truly maximize the firm's
resources and raise the bar on its performance. Given the fact
that Smythe's partners, associates, and administrators have to
work together (one conducts discovery, one prepares briefs,
another litigates, and still another bills clients), it is only logical
that a better understanding of how the work flows between
them and what can be done to eliminate redundancy and bol-
ster synergies will have a profound impact on productivity.
This holds true for every knowledge work environment.

The Power of Sound Decision Making

With this in mind, let's review another key component of the
invisible assembly line: the need for all of the people involved
to make intelligent decisions in the context of interdependence.
At Henry Ford's Highland Park factory, workers' tasks were
simple and rote: Turn a screw, tighten a belt, mount a door. In
the modern workplace, especially the knowledge-work environment, the requisite tasks are far more complex. In most
cases, decision making takes the place of, or is integrated with,
simple tasks. Because this book is designed to enhance individual and collective capabilities in the modern workplace, we
must take time to examine the components of decision making
and to sharpen our skills.

On any given day, in every workplace, knowledge workers
are called on to make hundreds of decisions. In the process,
most of us rely on vague or undefined means of arriving at
decisions, rather than using a systematic approach. If you and
your company are to achieve higher levels of productivity in
today's complex and rapidly changing environment, this is unacceptable. As Peter Drucker has warned, "decision-making
can no longer be improvised."

Let's take a look at the psychology and the habits that prevent the typical improviser from being a sound and effective
decision maker.

The Decision-Making Trap: Psychological Aspects

Panic

Often people recognize that a decision has to be made, but even when the issue is pressing, they want time to mull over every variable endlessly. In the vacuum created by this delay, conditions deteriorate. Suddenly, a decision has to be made in a panic mode. Because people function on an interdependent basis, this has negative repercussions across the assembly line.

Prejudice

In many cases, people have their minds made up even before a decision is made. This bias distorts the decision-making process, prompting individuals to make decisions and then build a case for them.

For example, a job candidate for a position at a Fortune 500 company has a background limited to small and mid-size companies. The interviewer (a company department manager) thinks that small-business people are less effective because they lack a "big-business perspective." So he makes the decision not to hire the interviewee (who is actually a highly talented and motivated executive) and then justifies his decision on the basis of illogical reasoning. What do we have here? Bias prevents the department manager from recruiting the best person, thus depriving the company and its assembly line of the skills and experience it needs to achieve maximum productivity.

Uncertainty

This is often evidenced by seizing the first option that comes along. It stems from a desire to be calm and orderly, avoiding the uncertainty of the predecision stage.

Logic

We've all met "Rational Ron and Rhonda," who try to be thoroughly rational in everything they do. Because they agonize and intellectualize endlessly, their decisions are often late and weak, producing a pattern of indecisiveness that interrupts the flow of work. Precisely because of the interdependence that characterizes the knowledge-work environment (whether the assembly line is invisible or not), any type of poor decision making has a domino effect, causing damage not only to the decision maker, but to his or her co-workers as well.

The Decision-Making Trap: Habit Patterns

Procrastination

Think of this as the "thief of time"—the "I'll do it later" syndrome. Drucker identifies procrastination as the most common problem in decision making. In a typical but destructive pattern, the procrastinator delays endlessly, hoping that during this stalling action circumstances will change, obviating the need for a decision. Or (another hallmark of the true procrastinator) the person hopes that the flow of events will dictate a decision, freeing the individual from accountability.

The best strategy for turning procrastinators into effective decision makers is to identify issues that require decisions, prioritize them, and set written deadlines for making them.

Passing the Buck

This frees the indecisive person from accountability, but it also deprives him or her of the credit that goes hand-in-hand with good decision making. If this sounds like you, be aware that if you always pass the buck, it is hard to be praised and, in turn, to acquire the political capital that goes with it.

On a collective basis, buck passing defies the interdependence, the collaboration, that must characterize a highly productive company. It means that the people in the best position to make effective decisions fail to do so. When this happens, the company does not adequately prepare for or respond to change. The best solution for this lack of discipline is to draw clear lines of responsibility and put them in writing. This serves as a schematic for the proper functioning of the assembly line, outlining personal duties and reporting relationships. By carefully detailing who is responsible for what, these written lines of responsibility reduce the likelihood of logjams and lapses in the work flow.

Complacency

This is evident when people fail to see a threat or an opportunity, or deliberately ignore the telltale signs of each, thinking, "It doesn't mean anything to me or my company."

This "head-in-the-sand" mentality led to the deterioration of IBM in the 1980s. IBM's managers refused to believe that mainframes would succumb to PCs in an era of rapidly changing technology. Similar complacency nearly doomed General Motors when its executives failed to believe in the Japanese threat until the company's market share eroded to ominous levels. This mindset also characterizes small companies that fail to update their products and services in response to changing demand, leaving themselves vulnerable to aggressive competitors.

To help prevent this, survey your company and the competitive landscape every three months. Ask yourself, "Do I want to watch my career or my business deteriorate with the spector of 'If only I had acted when I had the opportunity to do so from a position of strength'?" This reality check should prompt you to act, perhaps changing your product mix or reengineering the assembly line to produce more goods of higher quality.

Rationalization

Learn to identify rationalization in all of its forms: denying consequences, minimizing disadvantages while playing up the advantages, blaming someone else.

You must recognize when you are starting to justify decisions in this fashion. The best approach is to seek feedback from someone you trust—a co-worker, a peer manager, or (if you run the company) a board of directors. Rationalization may increase your personal comfort level, but it will also prevent you from taking the decisive actions that are critical in an interdependent workplace.

To avoid being weighed down and sidetracked by poor decisions, consider these five essential components of sound decision making:

1. *Define the issues.* You might do this by challenging the status quo. Or the issues may arise as you engage in your strategic vision exercise.
2. *Gather information.* This information may be in the form of expert people as well as data that can help in the process.
3. *List the alternatives* that are generated by the information-gathering process.
4. *Screen and evaluate* the impact the alternatives will have on your strategy, and the costs associated with them. Also, prioritize the alternative courses of action in order of merit.
5. *Come to a decision.* This is where you will have to identify and avoid all the habitual and psychological barriers to effective decision making.

Now that we understand the process, let's put it into practice. Use the decision-maker form in Figure 6-1.

Once a decision has been made and has become part of your plans, it is time for the critical imperative: To stay committed. If you find yourself wavering, keep in mind the decision-making wisdom of author and psychoanalyst Dr. Theodore Rubin: "It is almost always the decision maker, and not the particular choice, that makes a decision work." That's why it is important for you and your team to get behind the decision and make it work!

In previous chapters, we began developing a personal strategic vision; in this chapter we have learned skills to help in the decision-making process. Now comes the really exciting part:

Figure 6-1. Decision-maker form.

| Subject/Decision: | Target Date: |
| | Decision Date: |

Definition of Issue/The Challenge:

Why is decision necessary?

Consequences of doing nothing?

Impact on Strategy

Period 1:	Period 2:	Period 3:

Decision Mind Map

(continues)

Figure 6-1   (Continued.)

Subject/Decision:		Target Date: Decision Date:
Data	◄ Information Needed ►	People
1.		
2.		
3.		
4.		
5.		

Alternatives:	Evaluation: Impact on Strategy	Cost	Priority

The Decision:

Initiate Project Planner ✓ [   ]   Time Activate Decision [   ]

Putting these strategies, dreams, and goals into action. The ultimate goal is to manage and implement them, and bring them to fruition in the context of an interdependent, knowledge worker environment. This is central to leveraging the energy and power of the invisible assembly line.

LEARNING TRANSFER

Write a brief statement encapsulating your strengths and weaknesses as identified during your work in this chapter.

_____

_____

_____

_____

_____

Managing and Implementing Strategy

No doubt you've heard the term *strategic management* defined a thousand different times in a thousand different ways. But we'll make it very simple: Strategic management is the month-to-month, day-to-day implementation of your strategic vision. This section will show you how to convert your goals into projects and how to manage them (see Figure 6-2).

Ten-Step Guide to Project Planning

Step 1 Identify the project and the target data from your strategic statements.

Step 2 Define the objective (be specific) and describe the expected result. Estimate the cost, and note the team assembly-line leader if applicable. You should also check that the project relates to strategy. Does it affect your strategic vision in a positive or a negative way?

Step 3   Brainstorm and break the project into bite-sized, manageable portions.
Step 4   Think through and discuss with other team members possible contingencies, challenges, and preventors and list them on the left-hand

Figure 6-2. Project-planner form.

No.	Primary Tasks ◄ Action Steps ► Related Tasks	I/We Will Need These Resources People/Equipment/Money/Facilities	Seq.	Days/ Hours	Start Date	Compln. Date

Expected Result:

Estimated Cost:

Strategy Check   *Team Leader:*

All Items Time Activated ✓   *Total Cost*   *Completion Date ►*

▼▼

Team Members			
Name and Phone	Action Description/Responsibility	Commit. Date	Compln. Date

Other Departments/Outside Involvement/Responsibility			

▼ Obstacle ▼	Contingency Planning	▼ Solution ▼

Result/Observation

▲▲

side of a clean sheet of paper. Then, on the right-hand side, seek a solution.

Step 5   Sequence your activities by working down the column, asking where in the list of priorities each task should be placed (e.g., does the second follow the first?).

Step 6   Review the project with team assembly-line members and define their roles and commitments. Note the dates for start and completion. Ensure that all people involved are fully informed and that each has a written copy of the plan.

Step 7   Estimate the duration of each activity in days or hours.

Step 8   Time-activate the steps and note on the written checklist.

Step 9   Evaluate the project often by checking the completion dates. Remember to check the team members' commitment dates. This helps to ensure that all members of the assembly line and those with the ability to affect its work function in tandem.

Step 10   On completion of the project, appraise it with all team members and note results and observations for future reference. This is the best way to correct shortcomings, reinforce strengths, and raise the bar on future performance and productivity.

Real-World Close Up

Recently a human resources consulting firm set out to market a new product: motivational booklets designed for use by corporations to encourage such winning qualities as teamwork, persistence, and creativity.

From the beginning, the firm recognized that the booklets, illustrated by young artists, were of high quality and held great promise in the marketplace. But management needed a methodology for selling the booklets to corporate buyers. Acknowledging that it faced a formidable task (in part because it was new to the business), the firm started by creating a formal project plan.

The following were among the plan's key features:

1. Knowing from experience that the managers and employees involved in the project would function at a higher level if they were presented with a timetable, the firm stated its intention of making its first significant sales in six months (January 1 of the new year). This prodded management and employees to act with a sense of urgency, thus helping to head off competitors who were poised to enter the market.

2. To make certain that the firm increased the power of its assembly line, management clearly defined the project's objectives (to gain a foothold in a new market and to profit from the sale of motivational booklets) so that everyone could see where the project was headed. Equally important, a leader was assigned, with responsibility for completing the project successfully, on time, and within budget.

3. A key part of the leader's duties was to coordinate the efforts of all the employees involved in the project, to motivate them, and to orchestrate their efforts so that they functioned as a team rather than as Lone Rangers.

To accomplish this, the leader held brainstorming sessions (as called for in the project plan), during which creative strategies for accomplishing goals were developed and responsibilities for the various component tasks were assigned. This assured that (1) everyone had a role to play, (2) everyone's role was clearly defined, and (3) the project leader was responsible for holding the team members accountable.

4. As a by-product of the brainstorming sessions, the firm came to the painful conclusion that its instinctive approach to marketing the booklets—through direct sale to corporate buyers—would be prohibitively expensive. Following the project planning approach, management focused on this obstacle, identifying it as a serious issue that would require a creative solution before the firm could proceed.

Utilizing the combined brainpower of the team, the firm generated a wide range of plausible solutions, and kept refining these ideas until the participants agreed on the most promising approach: Rather than marketing directly to end users, the firm would enlist the support of an industry champion (specifically, a major distributor or network of distributors) that was active in the motivational products business. Through revenue-sharing agreements, it would leverage the power of these distributor relationships to market the booklets, thus moving out of the starting gate from a position of strength.

5. At the conclusion of the initial brainstorming sessions — which moved beyond marketing tactics to booklet concepts, production logistics, and vendor selection — management prioritized the workload, making certain that the most critical tasks (such as identifying the appropriate distributors) were tackled first.

6. Next, management assigned each of the tasks to one or more team members, making sure to link responsibilities with personal talents and experience.

The assignment process harnessed the power of the firm's assembly line. With each team member assuming a specific function or series of functions, and with all the team members aware of their peers' responsibilities as well as their own, the team was organized to function as a cohesive unit, reinforcing rather than conflicting with one another's activities.

None of this coordination was left to chance. A master project calendar was drafted, detailing responsibilities and start and completion dates, and each team member was required to initial the overall plan as well as his or her personal duties.

7. Finally, management created mechanisms for monitoring and revising the firm's course as it moved ahead. As part of this process, the project participants were to meet as a group on a monthly basis, gauging progress, identifying problems, seeking solutions, and making midcourse corrections. All in all, the methodology was in place to achieve success in the marketplace through a highly productive team effort. Although marketing booklets represented a new business challenge, by adjusting and refining the existing assembly line, the firm was confident of achieving great success.

Benefits of Project Planning

- It eliminates surprise by planning in detail, including the consideration of all contingencies.
- It removes grey areas, such as whose job it is to perform a specific function. Every person involved becomes ac-

countable and responsible for his or her part of the project.
- It removes projects from skunk works and special categories and are incorporated in the assembly line, which should be monitored and managed carefully.
- It puts all the project information in one place and is accessible for speedy decisions.
- It provides an assembly-line schematic for achieving individual and collective goals. Thus, as the business seeks to adapt to change and thrive in it, all of the components (people, capital, resources) work in unison toward that objective.

Learning Review

Read through the learning review below and check those items that have particular relevance for you and/or your team. Once you have completed this, circle the *one item* that you feel has been a learning breakthrough and discuss its significance with your fellow participants.

- ☐ Planning and decision making are processes, and can be brought under control if we use logical, sequential thinking techniques.
- ☐ There are five logical steps in making a decision.
- ☐ Strategic statements written as goals can be made into projects.

LEARNING TRANSFER

Write a brief statement encapsulating your strengths and weaknesses as identified during your work in this chapter.

_____

_____

_____

_____

_____

7

Managing Priorities: Doing the Right Job at the Right Time

"The rule is jam tomorrow and jam yesterday—but never jam today."

—Lewis Carroll

Identifying the invisible assembly line and finding one's place in it is advantageous to the individual employee as well to the company.

To see why, let's return to the example of the Smythe, Smythe, & Smythe law firm. Assume that the firm bases individual compensation primarily on the amount of fee income the partner generates for the practice. In this context, partner Susan Green, who specializes in merger and acquisitions, is delighted when she lands a new client, a major retailer about to acquire a former competitor in a friendly takeover. Because this will generate substantial fees, this is a win/win proposition for Green and Smythe.

But winning the new client is only the beginning of the story. Then, the process of providing the necessary legal work begins. Basically, Green has three choices:

1. Play the client close to the vest by trying to do most of the work herself.
2. Search for isolated sources of expertise in the firm and

seek their assistance in performing segments of the work.

3. Utilize the invisible assembly line and employ it to perform and deliver the client services seamlessly. For this approach to work (and making it work should be a top priority), Green and her managing partner must engineer the assembly line to make certain that the appropriate professionals are in place to conduct research, discovery, litigation, billings, and promotion, and that these individuals function interdependently to harness the power of synergy.

Utilizing the assembly line in this way is beneficial for Smythe, Smythe, & Smythe because it helps the firm achieve the highest level of efficiency, profitability, and client satisfaction. It is also ideal for Green because it liberates her from being fully absorbed by a single engagement and simultaneously frees her to do what she does best: attract new clients to the firm. Again we have a win/win proposition. The firm maximizes the skills of one of its most productive rainmakers, and Green maximizes her earning potential by attracting an ever-greater number of clients to the practice.

Viewed in a broader context, engineering the invisible assembly line has enabled the individual and the firm to manage priorities. And the ability to manage priorities on a daily basis, as well as over the long term, is a key component of all knowledge work.

So far, our engineering process has helped you look at the future, determine the end product, and then work backward to establish a framework for achieving your goals. We now enter the next dimension of knowledge work, the ability to do the right job, not just do the job right! It is here that most of us come up short, constantly mistaking "urgent" for "important." But we should do everything in our power to avoid the "urgency trap." Managing priorities helps you steer a steady course toward higher production and competitive advantage, even when change is causing great volatility in the marketplace.

Why is this so? Because managing priorities enhances your

ability to alter your behavior and opinions in the light of new information or changing situations. This is not as simple as it seems. In today's environment, employees and managers must face key questions: How can you remain effective during rapidly changing assignments? What skills should you employ when working under tight deadlines? What should be eliminated from your schedule? What should be added? How do you handle the flow of information in an effective way?

The answer to these questions, summed up in a single word, is *planning*. As we proceed through this chapter, we shall see how planning is the key to effective, ongoing priority management.

Let's start by reviewing the major categories of prioritization.

The secret to highly effective behavior is an understanding of the *activities matrix* (see Figure 7-1). Put simply, this means your activities can be placed on an urgent/important matrix, resulting in four distinct quadrants:

• MI, *highly important and highly urgent quadrant*. These are *direct value-adding* activities, such as making a sale, conducting a staff presentation, or writing a report to a team leader. Many people live their lives here, perceiving all work as both urgent and important. If every activity is considered to be in this quadrant of the matrix, a crisis environment is likely to ensue. We feel that we are constantly putting out fires.

• MII, *values:* high-importance, low-urgency quadrant. These are *indirect value-adding* activities, such as learning a skill, creating a mission statement, or designing a measurement process. Typically, these activities are important but not urgent; they add great meaning to both our personal and our working lives over the long term, but not immediately. Because of their lack of immediacy, it is easy to procrastinate on activities (such as spending more time with a child or meeting with friends) that naturally fit this quadrant.

• MIII, *tyranny of the urgent quadrant*. This contains activities that are urgent but of small importance. Consider these *necessary non-value-adding* activities. Examples are filling out

Figure 7-1. Professional (work) matrix.

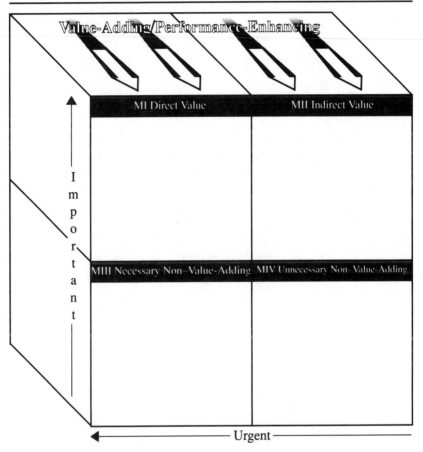

government documentation, taking "nuisance" phone calls, and correcting mistakes or defects that should have been detected at the source.

• *MIV, the busywork quadrant.* This is work that is of both low importance and low urgency. It tends to be where we go when we want to escape, often because work just gets to be too much. The problem is that some people find a comfortable niche here! This may be fine for the psyche, but it's a drag on productivity. These *unnecessary non-value-adding* activities include compiling information no one reads, engaging in trivia, and cleaning out your desk—again!

Note that the more time you spend in the MI and MII quadrants, the higher your performance level and the higher the value of your work will be. By adding depth to the important/ urgent and values quadrants, you can improve both the quantity and the quality of your work.

APPLICATION EXERCISE

On Figure 7-1, in each quadrant write three typical activities that you engage in during the course of your work. Be prepared to discuss them with a coworker, business associate, or board of directors. For each activity, ask, "Does this activity belong in the assigned quadrant? Is it commanding an inappropriate amount of your time? Would you be wiser to move it to another quadrant?" In answering these questions, first note the activity and then seek to justify it. If you cannot do so legitimately, seek to reposition it.

The following steps are designed to help you order your priorities as an effective knowledge worker by concentrating on quadrant MI and MII activities, both monthly and weekly.

1. Establish five monthly business goals (see Figure 7-2). These should be rather broad; do not confuse them with a daily "to do" list.
2. Engage in weekly development planning (see Figure 7-3) to ensure that your values, vision, and mission are translated into actions. These vitally important parts of your life can so easily become "if onlys" without this development planning process.

The assembly line cannot function effectively if the factory floor is untidy and littered. The same applies to your desk. Think of it as a factory where raw material (information) comes through one door, and a finished product (such as a report) goes out the other.

To be truly effective, you need to clear the clutter and associated desk stress and work on *one* project at a time. The following will help you avoid the pitfall of desk stress:

Figure 7-2. Monthly planner.

Priorities for Month ___November___ Year _____

Projects / Objectives

B	A	▼ Business ▼	Start Day	Result
	A	Completion of PAX project proposal	11/2	
	A	Inventory control modifications	11/21	
B		Year end staff evaluations	11/15	
	A	Quality inspection of overseas operations	11/1	
B		Staff party	11/3	

▼ Personal ▼

▼ Strengths ▼	Monthly Evaluation	▼ To Improve ▼

- Create three holding files and keep them close at hand. These three files are:
  1. Mail/correspondence
  2. Reading
  3. Projects/miscellaneous
- Remove all items from your desk and place them in four categories:
  1. Discard
  2. To file
  3. Can wait or delegate
  4. Act on

- Work through the act-on pile and make decisions as to when to do each item (i.e., time-activate) and also as to where the information is to be kept (holding files, etc.) Next, go to your *can wait* or *delegate* pile and treat it the same way as the *act-on* pile.
- Remember to clear your desk at the end of every working day. If you start the day with a cluttered desk, it's hard to keep on target.

Don't become a victim of desk stress. The top executives of the top corporations do not work from messy desks. They can't afford to sit and look at billion-dollar headaches day and night. A common denominator of the top CEOs (maybe the only one) is that they work from a clean desk—you can too!

Figure 7-3. Weekly development strategy planner.

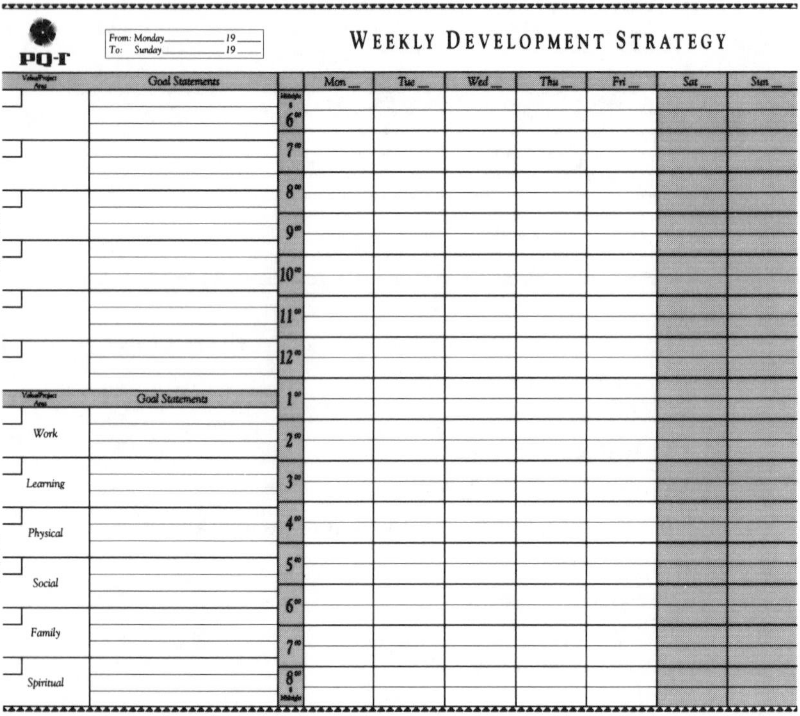

Defining Performance Expectations
(Q² Factoring) Evaluation

PQ-I

Organizational	Score		Process - Value Matrix		Notes

HIGH — HIGH

M I	Direct Value	M II	Indirect Value

PERFORMANCE — IMPORTANCE

A's

M III	Necessary Non-Value	M IV	Unnecessary Non-Value

B's

LOW — LOW

Total

Personal	Score	Balance Wheel	Notes

Work — Learning — Personal Values — Physical — Social — Family — Spiritual

Total

The Importance of
Communications/Delegation

In an interdependent workplace, especially one in which change must be identified and adapted to rapidly, strong communication skills are of critical importance. That's because getting things accomplished quickly (think of time as a competitive standard) often requires immediate and informal communication. What's more, learning—the most important skill of the new knowledge economy—is enhanced by effective communication. It helps to make certain that the sound decision-making process we worked on in Chapter 6 is put to good use in initiating actions across the assembly line and, in turn, throughout the company.

As you focus on communication skills, bear in mind that they are critical to effective delegation, which is vital for completing projects in order of priority. When people attempt to do it all themselves, interdependence—a key feature of the assembly line—is jeopardized. Attorney Green recognized this when she delegated parts of the bankruptcy case throughout the Smythe, Smythe, & Smythe firm. For people in the workplace to function effectively as a team, delegation and empowerment must be encouraged throughout the organization. Communication serves as the conduit for assigning and continually redefining power and responsibility.

We have already examined empowerment. Now let's look at the steps essential to effective delegation:

1. *Plan before you delegate.* Don't delegate what you can eliminate. Respect the obligations and abilities of others, and don't waste their time on trivial items. If possible, give multiple delegations at one time.

2. *Decide who does it.* Don't skip levels without checking first. Always consult a person's supervisor before delegating to that person. Remember to show *situational awareness*—the person may need more or less coaching to handle the assignment depending on his or her experience with the subject matter.

3. *Communicate the details.* Describe what is being delegated, and tailor the message to the individual. Give enough information to enable the delegatee to carry out the assignment. Eliminate potential confusion over the timing for follow-up activities by setting deadline dates.

Whenever possible, hand over what you are delegating in person. This enables you to talk over *how* the work is to be done, *who* does what, and *when* the results are expected.

Equally important, make sure that you delegate *authority* as well as *responsibility*. This means that once a project is assigned and you have established controls and checks, leave the delegatee to get on with it.

4. *Manage and evaluate.* Remember to establish times for review and schedule the reviews. Leave no doubt as to what you expect to be achieved by the review date. Resist the tendency for the assignments (or parts of them) to be delegated back to you!

5. *Reward successful completion* of all work finished on target and on time. Praise can often be the most effective reward. Try a handwritten note of "Thanks" for a job well done.

For unsuccessful assignments, or those that are only partially successful, identify errors and shape a positive approach for the future.

Real-World Close-Up

Here is another example of the powerful payoff that can come through the process of delegation. Like many of his peers in the senior management community, the CEO of a Montreal-based company specializing in office building safety measures believed that he was strong in all the basic leadership disciplines. That was before he was convinced to complete a Priority Management's Process-Skills Analysis, which analyzes and rates an individual's competencies. Much to the executive's shock, he had poor results in each of the key areas, including an inability to make clear and effective decisions.

After admitting that he needed help (a critical starting point of the improvement process) and engaging in a series of Priority Management training sessions designed to improve his performance in all the core competencies, he decided to make significant changes in his modus operandi. Not the least of these was to incorporate a management tool, the Decision Maker and Project Planner (Figures 6-1 and 6-2), that can guide all of the participants in an assembly line in the most effective and productive way to make decisions, conduct a project, or fulfill responsibilities.

Immediately, the Decision Maker proved its value. Purely by coincidence, at the time the P-SA training began, the company had scheduled a critical meeting with a prospective client—a leading office building management firm—in London. At the outset, the CEO had planned to make the trip himself, as he believed that he should handle the initial sales pitch with all significant prospects. But as he worked through the Decision Maker exercise, it became apparent that his sales manager had the best track record in dealing with leads and, given that he was a native of the United Kingdom, had an advantage that would and should be applied to the opportunity at hand.

Putting ego aside, the CEO passed the ball to the sales manager and focused instead on a major headquarters-based assignment that demanded close attention. As it turned out, all of the pieces fell neatly into place. Doing what the data indicated he had done time and again, the sales manager made a strong impression on the prospect, laying the foundation for a $1.2 million contract that was signed in less than a month. And the CEO, free to tend to the home fires, put the finishing touches on an employee profit-sharing plan that bolstered morale and assured the retention of key employees who had been courted by competitors.

As is the case with every well-oiled assembly line, the participants did the right job, at the right time—and they and the company reaped the benefits, individually and collectively.

Real-World Close-Up

All too often, failure to delegate effectively is viewed as a personal shortcoming that threatens a manager's reputation but poses little threat to the business. Nothing could be further from the truth.

To comprehend the importance of effective delegation, let's explore a case example in a small business environment, where all of the elements (and their impact on one another) come clearly into focus.

In 1992, Catherine L., a successful life insurance agent, graduated from salesperson to entrepreneur by purchasing a local insurance brokerage firm. The agency, situated in an upscale suburban Chicago community, was poised for substantial sales and profits, but had consistently fallen short of its potential. Thus it sold for a bargain price.

Based on her broad experience in the insurance business, Catherine identified the root cause of the agency's disappointing performance, and developed a plan for capturing its full potential. Surprisingly, it all boiled down to a matter of delegation.

A little background is in order. The previous owner (suffering from a classic entrepreneurial handicap) had found it painful to delegate anything to anyone. Determined to perform every sales and administrative function singlehandedly, he defaulted on major sales prospects (by refusing to allow subordinates to serve them) and squandered valuable time that would have been far more productively focused on sales and marketing on performing clerical functions (including paying all of the company's bills).

From the start, Catherine took a dramatically different approach. Recognizing that her strongest talents were in courting and closing clients—many of whom would purchase large insurance contracts, generating substantial premiums—she hired a small but experienced office staff, freeing her to stay in the field landing lucrative business. And to cultivate modest prospects (clients who might begin by purchasing small policies but could graduate to ever-larger policies over the years), she hired a sales assistant and authorized him to comb the market for business opportunities.

With her staff in place, Catherine developed a method of delegating work and responsibilities that was designed to harness the power of her agency's assembly line and achieve maximum productivity:

• Instead of simply issuing edicts ("Smith, do this; Jones, do that"), Catherine encouraged her employees to volunteer for assignments that appealed to them, and that they believed they would perform well. Although there was never a guarantee that they would gain these prized assignments, if Catherine was convinced that there was a match between an employee's skills and the job at hand, she would flash the green light for a trial run. Although employees were still required to perform their basic duties, the opportunity to expand in new directions raised morale and gave the company, and its employees, the opportunity to achieve accelerated growth.

Should you seek to imitate Catherine's policy, remember to make the input for the delegation process bottom-up as well as top-down.

• Employees were never simply *told* to do something; they were *taught* to do it.

This addresses a familiar problem, one that often proves to be the Achilles heel of delegation. When managers assign work, they expect it to be performed in a certain way. However, they often leave employees guessing at what, specifically, they have in mind. This throws elements of the assembly line out of whack, prompts disappointment in the employees' performance, and ultimately leads to frustration with the entire delegation process.

To circumvent this negative turn of events at the outset, Catherine never simply ordered her employees to do something, she mentored them. For example, rather than simply cutting her young sales associate loose to brave the trials and tribulations of the marketplace, she asked him to accompany her on sales calls, so that he could observe—and learn from— an experienced hand at work. Reflecting this philosophy of continuous learning, Catherine asked each veteran employee to mentor the newcomers reporting to him or her. In this way, the company applied its collective wisdom to new members of the team, imparted the assembly-line perspective from the outset (because it was part of the veteran employees' mind-set), and greatly reduced the learning curve that often disrupts companies on a fast-growth track.

• Catherine took the time to truly reward and compliment deserving employees for a job well done. This involved more than a perfunctory pat on the back. She used creative touches to communicate clearly that she really comprehended and appreciated the employees' contributions. For example, Catherine sent handwritten notes to employees' homes, including a check for "dinner for two" on the company. The clear link between performance and reward added an extra dimension to the delegation process. In this environment, people were no longer working for a boss, they were working for a team.

Learning Review

Read through the learning review below and check those items that have particular relevance for you and/or your team. Once you have completed this, circle the *one item* that you feel has been a "Learning Breakthrough" for you, and discuss its significance with your fellow participants.

☐ Planning and communication tools can increase your productivity, quality, and interdependence.

☐ Results that are recognized get repeated. There is a five-stage delegation process.

☐ A clear desk can be a launchpad for increased productivity.

☐ Activities are both important and/or urgent, and we should differentiate between the two.

☐ We should try not to create "busywork" with available technology, but always ensure that the tools fit the work.

Personal Worksheet

1. Choose an activity you wish to delegate.
2. Choose the delegatee.
3. Prepare written communications on the delegation (be situationally aware).
4. Time-activate the delegation and follow up.

LEARNING TRANSFER

Write a brief statement encapsulating your strengths and weaknesses as identified during your work in this chapter.

_____

_____

_____

_____

_____

8

The Defining Performance Expectations (Q² Factoring) Performance Measurement Process

"Only a mediocre person is always at his best."

—W. Somerset Maugham

In business—any business—the marketplace is the ultimate test of individual and collective performance. Just how you fare against the competition and how your results vary from quarter to quarter and year to year speak volumes about how well (or poorly) you are structured to provide products and/or services. But waiting for the marketplace to measure performance can be fatal, because if you discover at that point that your performance is subpar, your career or your company may be at risk. That's why you need internal measurement systems in place, gauging your performance on an ongoing basis.

It has long been understood that measurement systems strongly affect people's behavior. At school, on the playing field, or in the office, measuring sets benchmarks, creates standards, and spurs initiative (to set new standards). On the track, for example, would sprinters achieve world-record performance if there were no stopwatches or gold medals? Of course not. Would the developed countries' industrial productivity have risen as dramatically over the past hundred years had we not measured the widgets per hour? Of course not.

But there is a problem in this measurement–performance relationship. We tend to measure productivity in the traditional arena of manual production work, but not in the increasingly important arena of knowledge work. So, in effect, we continue to encourage higher levels of productivity where it now matters least: Only 20 percent of people are now working in the widget per hour category, and they continue to make productivity improvements of 3 to 4 percent each year. The other 80 percent of the workforce is knowledge workers, but because there are no tangible widgets to measure their productivity, virtually no measurement is carried out. Without this measurement activity, the ability to achieve higher levels of knowledge worker performance is diminished.

That's the bad news. The good news is that while measurement of knowledge work is not as straightforward as measurement of widgets per hour, it is quite doable and, in fact, is essential for the proper functioning of your assembly line. This chapter presents an innovative approach to measuring knowledge-work performance, and thus provides a critical element for engineering the assembly line and ultimately raising the productivity of your organizations.

Measurement Systems: A Review

Traditional measurement systems evolved from financial functions and have their roots in organizational control. Typically, they say what the employee should do and then take measurements to see if the employee lives up to the boss's commands. These systems—an offshoot of the mass-production era—attempt to *control* behavior in the workplace. Everyone is treated as a faceless automaton with a certain number of widgets to produce.

The new information era in which we are all functioning

and competing demands a dramatically different approach, one that respects the individuality of each type of worker and puts strategy and vision at the core of the measurement process. Think of it this way: (1) You determine what must be done to satisfy the customer; (2) based on this knowledge, strategy is developed; and (3) the worker is empowered to adopt the appropriate behavior and activities to accomplish the strategy.

The *Defining Performance Expectations (Q² Factoring) measurement process,* one of the key components of the productive assembly line, addresses the delicate balance between *quantity* and *quality* and is designed to pull people toward the company's collective vision while respecting individual values. This duality is achieved by allowing each knowledge worker the latitude to be creative in arriving at desired outcomes in the constantly changing work environment. In this way, actions are not rote, but instead are tailor-made for each situation. This is the best way to assure that your line, unlike Henry Ford's, is flexible and adaptive, making it ideal for today's volatile markets and business conditions. As the saying goes, "People forget how fast you did a job—but they remember how well you did it."

As you pursue heightened productivity, the Performance Measurement Process will prove invaluable. Put simply, this is an ongoing process to measure, and in time improve, personal and organizational performance. Consider the key steps in the process (see Figure 8-1):

- *Step one:* Who is the customer for my work?
- *Step two:* What is the value of my work?
- *Step three:* How does the customer see me?
- *Step four:* What are my performance goals and how are they measured?
- *Step five:* What is the evaluation of my measurement process?

Step One: Who Is the Customer for My Work?

Every *k*-worker (knowledge worker) provides either a service or a product to one or more customers. In some cases, it is quite

Figure 8-1. Defining Performance Expectations (Q² Factoring) performance measurement process.

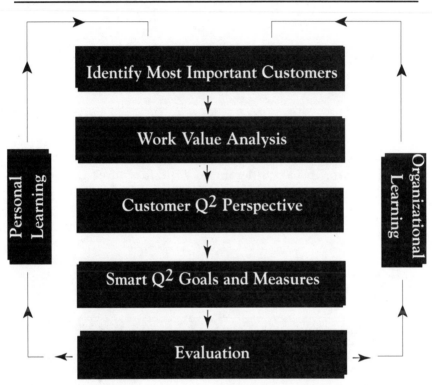

clear who the customer is. For example, a bank teller calls "next," the customer arrives and the service is performed. Because *k*-work output is so often another *k*-worker's input, sometimes we're not quite sure who the customer is, especially if it's someone within the same department, team, or organization. This first exercise is designed to ensure that you know who your customer is. It is only then that the measurement process can begin—with a customer focus.

In this exercise, you will analyze a *typical* day or period. Look back through your organizer *(Priority Management Systems)* to what you consider to be a typical day(s). If it was yesterday, all the better. You'll have a fresher memory.

How to Complete a Defining Performance Expectations (Q² Factoring) Customer Analysis

This form is in two parts (see Figure 8-2). First, the work/activities analysis ("Data").

Part One

Look at a typical day or several days' activities, both in and out of the workplace, and complete the first three columns of the Defining Performance Expectations (Q² Factoring) Customer Analysis.

Figure 8-2. Defining Performance Expectations (Q² Factoring) Customer Analysis.

DATA			VALUE ANALYSIS	
Activities/Work Area	Customer	Time	Most Important Customer/ Teams/People	Internal/ External
1. Marketing Meeting	Marketing Team	1.5	Rob	I
2. Read HBR Article	Rob	1.0	John	E
3. Draft of LMG Proposal	Wendy	2.0	Marketing Team	I
4. Set up Conference Call	Rob	.2		
5. Conference Call	Rob	1.0		
6. Meeting with Fred	Fred	.5		
7. Staff Meeting	Rob	1.0		
8. Call to Dan	Dan	.6		
9. Meeting with Wendy	Wendy	.5		
10.				

DATA			VALUE ANALYSIS	
Activities/Work Area	Customer	Time	Most Important Customer/ Teams/People	Internal/ External
1.				
2.				
3.				
4.				
5.				
6.				
7.				
8.				
9.				
10.				
11.				
12.				
13.				
14.				
15.				
16.				
17.				
18.				

1. List all of the activities/work for the given period of time under "Activities/Work Area."
2. Identify the customer/recipient of each of the activities under "Customer."
3. Enter the approximate time spent on the activity under "Time."

Part Two

Now, review your list of customers ("Value Analysis").
Who are the most important? List them under "Most Important
Customers/Teams/People." Reflect on the strategic statements
you developed in Chapter 5. Who are the recipients of that strategic activity? Should they be added to your list? As you reflect,
other key recipients of your work will come to mind. Add them
to your list. Ideally, identify your six to ten *most important* customers. Are these people internal (I) or external (E) customers?

Do the same for your personal life: Identify the most important activities and the most important people on the reverse
side of the Defining Performance Expectations (Q^2 Factoring)
Customer Analysis (Figure 8-2).

Step Two: What Is the Value of My Work?

Once you have analyzed a typical day and determined your
most important work, products, services, and customers, and
the time you typically give them, you can move into a value
analysis.

In the value column of the Value Analysis form, classify
each of your activities as MI, MII, MIII, or MIV (for a refresher
from the previous chapter, see Figure 8-3 for guidance).

Analyze the time spent in each of the four quadrant areas.
Express it in approximate hours and/or as a percentage of your
day and complete Figure 8-4.

Now it is time to arrive at some conclusions. With this in
mind, write a summary statement that reflects your analysis
of the value of your work on a typical day. Focus here on
an objective analysis of whether or not you are devoting
your skills and expertise to tasks that are of the "highest and
best use" as measured by their contribution to achieving the
company's goals.

_____

_____

Figure 8-3. Matrix for value column of the Value Analysis form.

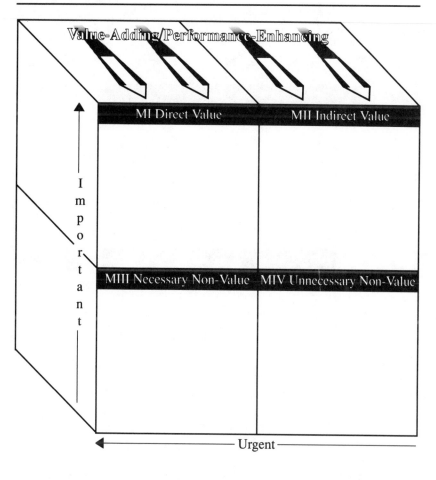

Step Three: How Does the Customer See Me?

Determining how you and your company perform from the customers' perspective must be a top priority. For this reason,

Figure 8-4. Time record matrix.

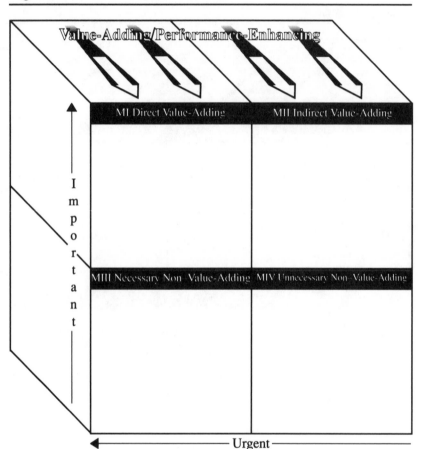

the Performance Measurement Process demands that you translate general or vague missions into specifics that really matter to your customers—be they team members or those who purchase your goods and services. With this in mind, this phase of our productivity process measures not only the volume (quantity), but also the quality of your work *as seen through the eyes of the customer*.

The objective of this exercise is to identify (preferably with the customer's input) a set of performance objectives that put the customer first. To give you critical insight, we will use another innovative component of our measurement process, the *Customer Perspective Analysis* (see Figure 8-5). This helps you explore the world from the viewpoint of the customer, providing another assurance that the measurement of your assembly line's performance is not abstract but instead real-world oriented.

Before you start on the Customer Perspective Analysis, note the following: This exercise is critical for improving your knowledge-factor effectiveness. The columns and spaces provided are designed to trigger the appropriate dialogue and processes to enable you to arrive at an achievable set of performance goals and measures in each critical area. (Annotations in the columns will suffice and serve as reminders of expectations.)

Proceed this way:

• In column I, write the names of your most important customers.

• In column II, write the quantity of goods or the amount of work the customer is ordering. (Remember: Your customer may be a colleague or your boss.)

• Quality is usually thought of in terms of the number of errors made (or not made) in the performance of your work. Your boss may just require a draft proposal at this stage. The quality of your work, then, should always be seen from the customer's viewpoint—not your own guess as to what is expected. This should be noted in Column III. Keep in mind that as a general rule, the later in the work process that errors are identified, the more expensive it is to correct them. This is especially true for knowledge work, which involves complex problems and solutions as well as a high degree of interdependence. Knowledge work errors at one stage of the assembly line can have serious implications for the end product. Addressing these errors after the fact is for more complicated than simply replacing a defective part. That's why for knowledge workers, the rallying cry must be, "Do it right the first time or you will have to find more time to do it again!"

• Column IV asks what lead time is expected, when projects are due, and how much time should be spent in each key

Figure 8-5. Defining Performance Expectations (Q² Factoring) Customer Perspective Analysis.

Name:				Date:	
I Most Important Customers	II Quantity	III Quality	IV Time/Timeliness	V Creativity	VI Interdependence

area of work. This is designed to draw attention to factors that influence the cycle time of products and services.

• Column V inquires about the degree of creativity or innovation that is expected.

• Column VI asks for agreement on the ways in which team members will work together: reporting, communication, interpersonal processes. By revealing interdependencies, this simple agreement identifies the invisible assembly line and creates the opportunity for engineering even in those companies (and among those individuals) with the most stubborn resistance to the concept. (Remember, revealing the existence of the assembly line approach to all workers, and helping individuals and organizations leverage it to achieve maximum productivity, is the major benefit of this book. In most cases, achieving this and maximizing the performance gains it will deliver will require a variety of approaches.)

Don't make the mistake of considering the Customer Perspective Analysis to be an isolated exercise. It should become part of your monthly/quarterly planning sessions. It can be conducted personally or as a group activity with a team.

Real-World Close-Up

A successful Boston-based travel agency tackles the customer perspective, and its impact on quality, through an innovative process that starts by moving outside the internal perspective and into the minds of its clients.

As specialists in upscale executive travel—arranging for business and pleasure voyages—the agency serves a highly discriminating clientele. This leaves little margin for error. When destinations, hotels, limousines services, and the like are recommended by the agency's consultants, they must provide the level of excellence the agency's clients demand. To achieve this quality control, the agency builds in two fail-safe measures:

1. At least two of the agency's consultants must visit the sight or use the service and be completely delighted with it before it qualifies for the agency's recommended list.

2. Agency consultants require the management of each site or service to provide references from customers who are demographically similar to the agency's own client list. These customers are then interviewed by telephone to gain their perspective on the quality issue. Questions include: "Did the property fall below, satisfy, or exceed your expectations? Did you experience service flaws or lapses that would make you think twice before returning?" (Even when the vendor hand-picks referral sources, penetrating questions tend to produce candid responses.)

Once the field research has been collected, it is shared with the entire staff, management and consultants—not in the standard memos that make their way around run-of-the-mill travel agencies, but in "client perspective workshops" held every Friday morning in the agency's conference room.

At these colorful and informal sessions, consultants returning from field trips relate details of their research, presenting personal travel logs covering food, service, furnishings, and special appointments. Equally important, the consultants reveal the outcome of their referral research, offering the highly personal perspective of executive ratings. This transforms the appraisal process from a superficial view to a revealing glimpse into the real world of the customer.

Clearly, the process takes time and requires consultants to devote some of the hours in which they could be selling and booking travel to individual and collective research. But for a company with a demanding and sophisticated customer base, and a mandate to deliver an exceptionally high level of performance, quality research provides a high return on investments, measured in terms of customer satisfaction and extraordinary loyalty.

Step Four: What Are My Performance Goals and How Are They Measured?

Through a combination of self-analysis and dialogue (again note the importance of communications) with associates and principal customers, you are now ready to establish key performance goals and measures to support these objectives.

To refresh your memory, when declaring goals or strategic statements, it is important to make them *S.M.A.R.T.*:

- Specific
- Measurable
- Attainable
- Relevant
- Trackable

You have all of the information you need to make your performance goals *S.M.A.R.T.* and measurable. That's because by now they have been designed to have the greatest impact on customer satisfaction, including such factors as cycle time, productivity, quality, and creativity.

Note on Measures

The measurements used by knowledge workers must make sense to both the employees and management. If they do not, the primary objective of the measurement process, to improve performance, is unlikely to be met.

With this in mind, remember that the measurement tool is not a weapon to be used against an individual or a team. Instead, it should serve as a motivator to enhance results. If your goals have been generated through discussion among colleagues, associates, supervisors, and external customers, the best measures will come from these sources.

Another key point: Although knowledge work is complex, it is not a good idea to have more than a few key measures for each goal; we advise three or four. Any more, and priorities will become confused; any less, and the goals may not be adequately measured.

We call this process of establishing multiple measures for our goals the *invisible assembly-line family of measures*. "Invisible assembly line" reminds you that goals will be driven by productivity factors, quality factors (such as timeliness), and interpersonal factors (such as teamwork), and "family of measures" reminds you that more than one measure is appropriate because it supports a holistic approach.

Monthly or quarterly evaluation is a critical part of the Defining Performance Expectations (Q^2 Factoring) measurement process. It should not be used as a couch for resting on or as a tool for beating up on yourself or another person, but as a platform or benchmark for enchanced future performance.

Summarize your ongoing evaluations, noting in brief both areas of strength (celebrate!) and areas for improvement (commit yourself to this). This evaluation should be both individual and collective for all members of the assembly line.

_____

_____

_____

_____

_____

_____

_____

_____

As you (and your teams) apply the measurement process, you will see a fundamental shift in the underlying assumptions about performance measurement. Specifically, the process does not emphasize control, but rather puts strategy and vision at its core. As such, it is designed to pull everyone toward the overall vision of the organization, to identify weaknesses in the assembly line, to create benchmarks, and to establish a framework for increasing productivity.

At the end of the month or quarter, the example results can be analyzed using the family of measures approach on the Defining Performance Expectations (Q^2 Factoring) Measurement Process Form (see Figure 8-6).

Figure 8-6. Defining Performance Expectations (Q² Factoring) Measurement Process form.

Name (Person/Team): Sandy Johnson				Month/Qtr.: 3rd Quarter 19	
I	**II**	**III**	**IV**	**V**	**VI**
1. Goal/Project	*Benchmark*	*Result*	*Result/Benchmark*	*Weighting*	*Weighted Result*
A. 10% More Proposals	20	23	115%	.40	46
B. More Timely	80	85	106%	.20	21
C. Fewer Mistakes	95	90	95%	.40	38
				1.00	105

The Defining Performance Expectations (Q² Factoring) Measurement Process Form

Column 1 is a summary statement of the goals to be achieved.

In column II, the benchmark is the approximation of what is normal for the measure. In our example (Figure 8-7), the person usually generates twenty proposals a quarter: 80 percent on time and with 95 percent accuracy.

Column III shows the result recorded after a month (or quarter).

Column IV is the result divided by the benchmark (norm). We see that at the end of the period, 15 percent more proposals were generated, 6 percent improvement of on-time performance, but mistakes were 5 percent worse.

Column V shows the weights we assigned each part of the goal at the beginning of the month (quarter).

Column VI shows whether the weighted average shows an increase or decrease in the result. This is calculated by multiplying the new benchmark value by its assigned weight (115 × 40 percent). This gives the actual weighted result, and by adding them, we see that Sandy Johnson scored 105, which is a 5 percent overall improvement for this goal.

In order to assure the best possible Defining Performance

Figure 8-7. Defining Performance Expectations (Q² Factoring) Measurement Process.

Name (Person / Team): Sandy Johnson				Month/Qtr.: 3rd Quarter	
				19	
I	II	III	IV	V	VI
1. Goal / Project	Benchmark	Result	Result / Benchmark	Weighting	Weighted Result
A. 10% More Proposals	20	23	115%	.40	46
B. More timely	80	85	106%	.20	21
C. Fewer Mistakes	95	90	95%	.40	38
				1.00	105

Expectations (Q² Factoring) factor performance along the assembly line, managers and supervisors may identify a need to assess their employees' key strengths and weaknesses. Having an accurate picture of who does what best can prove invaluable in assigning responsibilities and measuring performance.

That's where Priority Management Process-Skills Analysis can serve as an exceptional tool, especially when combined with an innovative approach key to raising performance levels.

Consider the experience of an electronic parts distributor whose general manager required fifty-two employees responsible for conducting the company's business at a key distribution center to engage in the Process-Skills Analysis.

Once the results were in hand, employees were informed of their weak points (in an instructive rather than a threatening way) and coached on ways to improve their performance.

While many companies might stop there, considering the process complete, the distributor went a critical step further, announcing that employees would be required to go through the Process-Skills Analysis a second time. At that point, improvements in performance would be noted and rewarded.

Staff response proved positive from the start. Cognizant of the fact that a higher caliber of work would be identified, and appreciative that their extra efforts would result in raises and bonuses, they made (and continue to make) a determined effort to raise the bar on the quality and quantity of the company's distribution services. Consider it an ongoing benchmarking process, designed to identify Defining Performance Expectations (Q² Factoring) performance levels and produce continuous improvement in both the quantity and quality components.

Step Five: What Is the Evaluation of My Measurement Process?

As we have noted, engineering the invisible assembly line is an individual as well as a collective process. The Weekly Development Strategy Planner (Figure 7-3) can help you take a proactive role in raising the level of your performance, increasing your value to the company, and, in turn, enhancing your career. This form puts personal vision and strategy along with organizational objectives at the forefront of your agenda. At the end of a week, and before planning your next week's activities, review the week gone by and note your organizational and personal successes. For example:

- Did you achieve the planned balance and live up to your matrix goals for the week—that is, did you spend a large percentage of your time in MI and MII activities?
- Make a note of your challenges to be addressed and next week's matrix goals.
- Did you identify the most valued customers for your work?
- How did customers see you? Score 1 (badly) to 10 (exceeded their expectations).

One of the most effective ways to use your Weekly Development Strategy Planner is to gradually move as many of your activities as possible out of MIII and MIV and into the high-value-adding quadrants MI and MII. Start the week by writing a goal statement for each quadrant in the process-values matrix. For example, for MI, you may well decide that "meeting with a client" is a direct value-adding activity. In MIV, you might write "attending business etiquette seminars" as an unnecessary, non-value-adding activity. These statements are reminders only, and are designed to help you stay focused on high-quality, high-performance goals for the next week.

Weekly evaluation will help you achieve your monthly and quarterly goals by keeping you targeted.

Learning Review

Read through the learning review below and check those items that have particular relevance for you and/or your team. Once you have completed this, circle the *one item* that you feel has been a learning breakthrough, and discuss its significance with a colleague or friend.

☐ The measurement process is designed for knowledge workers and is used as a way to pull people toward their vision.

☐ Every knowledge worker provides a service or product to one or more customers. It is essential to know who the most important customers are.

☐ By analyzing time and activities, it is possible to estimate whether time is spent in high-value or low-value activities.

☐ Knowing what both internal and external customers expect before setting performance objectives is key.

☐ Performance goals and measures should be set and monitored weekly, monthly, and quarterly.

LEARNING TRANSFER

Write a brief statement encapsulating your strengths and weaknesses as identified during your work in this chapter.

_____

_____

_____

_____

_____

_____

_____

_____

9

Taking Ownership, Responsibility, and Accountability: Power to the People

"In knowledge and service work, partnership with the responsible worker is the only way to increase productivity."

—Peter Drucker

At this point, we have set performance goals and begun the measurement process, but these goals and objectives are only as good as your commitment to them and to the larger vision and values of your organization. This leads us to a critical question: Are you committed to these goals and objectives, or are you merely involved? Considering the challenges you and your company face in identifying and engineering the assembly line for maximum productivity in the knowledge workplace, mere involvement is not sufficient. You had better be fully committed.

This reflects the fact that in today's environment, you will have to do more than ever before. The pace of change in the information era, and the competitive force it unleashes, requires knowledge workers to assume leadership roles outside of their formal assignments. This so-called skills convergence (see Figure 9-1) occurs as organizations flatten and managers

Figure 9-1. Skills convergence.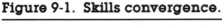

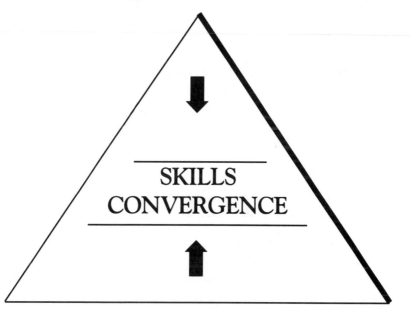

surrender some degree of independent behavior and decision making to nonsupervisory staff. Visualize this as knowledge workers moving outside of their organizational boxes, both for their own good and for the good of the company.

Here's the key point: The ability to take ownership, assume responsibility, and be accountable for profits and losses—once the exclusive reserve of top management—can no longer be limited to senior executives. Taking ownership is essential for all high-performance, highly productive knowledge work. That's because it leads to a higher level of personal responsibility: Instead of shirking challenges or passing them off to others, employees act on the mind-set that "I have a stake in this." All across the assembly line, they are determined to get the job done.

What kind of behavior is required to face up to this responsibility? Having a *positive self-image* (i.e., believing in oneself), having *tenacity* (the ability to make repeated and enduring efforts to overcome obstacles and complete tasks), being *independent* (holding to your own convictions in the face of resistance), and having the ability to take the *initiative* (engaging in proactive behavior in order to seize opportunities).

Think of it this way: Are you waiting for someone to give you permission to own your work and career, or will you do it yourself? Visualize a young man anxiously pacing outside the door of the personnel manager. A wily old-timer, a veteran of the place, passes by and asks the lad what he is doing. "Waiting to see what they're planning for me," comes the reply. The old man, without missing a beat, replies, "Invest in yourself. If you don't, why should they?"

This chapter will help you make that investment.

The Partnering Process

For ownership of workplace projects and activities to be truly effective and generate significant productivity gains, it must extend from the individual to the team level, resulting in the formation of "productivity partnerships." These alliances are forged between those who share a stake in a project, activity, or assignment. Generally, these partnerships are created between supervisors and employees; however, in the most productive organizations, they are forged wherever there is work to be done—between colleagues, or between internal teams and outside agencies and vendors.

The goal of the *invisible assembly-line partnering process* is to build responsibility, ownership, and accountability into all major work goals, regardless of their level, difficulty, or skill. This building and constant reinforcing of the bonds between people united in pursuit of a common effort helps the company and its employees respond effectively to the shifting challenges of a changing business environment. The reason is simple: As demands and requirements change, employees who are simply doing a job remain on their original course, blaming their difficulties on events beyond their control. But employees who are infused with a sense of ownership, accountability, and interdependence, don't "blame." Instead, they seek to make course adjustments that will result in a successful outcome.

Case in point: In the midst of a recession, a large hotel

needed to reduce its housecleaning staff, spreading the same responsibilities over a smaller group of people. In other words, each maid would have to be more productive.

In order to tackle this challenge, management formed a "partnership" with the maids, soliciting their suggestions on how to solve the problem. Because only the maids knew both the extent of their jobs and their personal obligations outside the workplace, they were in the best position to develop a workable strategy. Their solution was to have the women take turns staying home and babysitting for all of the team's children while the others completed their expanded tasks. Instead of all of the employees having to hurry home to their children, they were able to devote the necessary time to complete the work without worrying about conflicting responsibilities. That's creativity—and the power of that is partnership. No group of "senior" managers, however talented, would ever have come up with this solution. The lesson is: No one knows the work as well as the person doing it. Have faith in the intelligence of the worker to come up with partnerships that are creative and intelligent!

Put simply, the partnering process is the establishment of, and commitment to, key performance goals by all of the participants on the assembly line. It commences with the setting of performance objectives and measures (as discussed in the preceding chapter) and moves on to establishing ownership, responsibility, and accountability (ORA).

The *Partnering Agreement* (see Figure 9-2) is designed to help the assembly-line participants in a project or ongoing assignment arrive at a mutual agreement concerning how and when the work will be done. The agreement serves two functions:

1. A road map for leading you or your team through a process
2. A guide to the partnering process, helping to ensure that the parties reach a proper understanding

In either case it can be completed as a formal agreement (signed by the respective individuals) or committed to on the basis of

Figure 9-2. Partnering agreement.

Strategic goal/work:			Target date:	
			◀ **Between** ▶	

Key objectives:	When	Consequences:
		▶
		▶
		▶
		▶
		▶
		▶
		Personal:
S☐ M☐ A☐ R☐ T☐		

Resources

People:	Equipment:	Money:	Time:

Action Steps | *Date*

Situational Awareness | *Date*

Interdependence:

Accountability: | *Follow up Date*

_____   _____   _____   _____
Signature   Date   Signature   Date

an oral pledge. Whether you choose to use it in written or oral form depends on the situation, experience, and interpersonal relationships of the individuals involved.

Establishing Ownership, Responsibility, and Accountability (ORA): The Partnering Agreement Process

Identify a key strategic goal, project, or work assignment. Identify the major stakeholders in the project and arrange a mutually agreeable time to meet with them.

Using the Partnering Agreement form, follow these steps:

1. Name the strategic goal, project, or work assignment, and together establish a target completion date.

2. Complete the "Between" information by naming the parties to the agreement. These may be teams or individuals.

3. Discuss and agree on the key objectives. Are they S.M.A.R.T.?

4. Agree on when each objective will be accomplished.

5. Agree on the consequences of the objectives. All projects involve a wide range of potential consequences. This part of the process is designed to review all of the possible repercussions, both positive and negative. The idea is to be prepared for all of the eventualities the team may face (another key element of effective management in a volatile business environment).

6. The "Resources" section establishes the people, equipment, time, and money issues surrounding the work. You should place emphasis on the time commitment. This is where knowledge-work partnerships often break down. That's because the parties don't agree on *when* their contributions to the project are due.

7. "Action steps" summarizes the key activities and guidelines that will ensure completion of the goal. The date column captures critical time frames that should serve as reference points for all the participants.

8. "Situational Awareness" will help you decide how much supervision is required. Leaders should take into account both the ability and the willingness of their colleagues to perform the scheduled duties. This helps to determine the level of guidance required for each project. A little background will prove useful here. Many supervisors/managers adopt one style of behavior for all occasions. This will typically be successful about 25 percent of the time. Recognizing the ability and willingness of the person with whom you are forging a partnership before deciding on your style of leadership for the assignment is a more effective approach.

9. Interdependence involves developing a plan to muster the people resources for the project. At this point, it is important to discuss anticipated time commitments and due dates.

10. In the final step of the partnering process, agreement on accountability must be achieved. A discussion should cover these key elements:

- Are you accountable for parts of the work?
- Which tasks?
- Do other individuals involved in the assembly line know of their parts?
- Have they taken accountability?
- Are you accountable for the overall project?
- If not, who is?

Quickly review the major steps of the partnering process and sign off. Keep a copy of the agreement where you can refer to it as the project proceeds. The key benefit of the partnering process is that it transfers the all-important "ownership" of the work to the appropriate knowledge workers on the assembly-line team. Keep in mind that in manufacturing work, partnership with the responsible worker is the *best* way to increase productivity. In knowledge and service work, partnership with the responsible worker is the *only* way.

You will find the Partnering Agreement to be the most effective tool you can use to bring about win-win situations among teams. Use one each time a major project is established.

Real-World Close-Up

Consider the positive impact of a well-crafted partnership agreement between three co-founders and key functional executives at Good Looks Apparel, Inc. (a fictitious name for a real New York–based sportswear firm).

The company was launched on a relatively simple premise: Stanley R., the major investor, would serve as a silent partner; Richard A., the creative guru, would be responsible for designing the firm's apparel line; and Diane K., a Wharton MBA with industry experience in the Calvin Klein organization, would serve as Good Looks general manager.

On the surface, this division of duties seemed clear and sensible. Each partner would assume ownership of the functional area most closely matching his or her skills and resources. Accordingly, each component of the assembly line had a skilled hand at the helm.

But while the organizational structure appeared ideal on paper, it quickly broke down in practice:

- Stanley, the self-proclaimed silent partner, proved to be anything but silent. He interrogated employees, challenged practices and questioned expenses, always threatening to cut off the flow of funds if the company failed to heed his directives.
- Richard was angry and frustrated over Stanley's meddling in the design process. "How," he would thunder, "can a man who knows nothing about fashion tell *me* how to design a clothing line?" Pushed to the brink, Richard was on the verge of leaving the business, without regard to the legal and financial consequences.
- As Diane discovered in short order, running a business in a highly competitive industry is difficult; simultaneously keeping warring partners at bay is virtually impossible. With her attention diverted from the marketplace, the company was in dire straits, struggling to survive.

Fortunately, Good Looks' accountant (who had heard endless gripes and threats from the three principals) recognized

that the company's fundamentals were sound: There was sufficient cash to keep the wheels turning, a strong creative force,
and a highly capable business manager. All that was lacking
was a means of effectively coordinating these critical components of the company's assembly line.

Guided by this insight (based on decades of experience
serving as a jack-of-all-trades advisor to entrepreneurial companies), the CPA demanded that the partners agree to a truce
and a summit meeting. Serving as the facilitator, he encouraged the principals to air their gripes (in what proved to be a
cathartic session) and then, with the slate clean, to agree that
each would play the role he or she had pledged to fill at the
outset—and, accordingly, would be free of undue interference
from the others. To make certain that no one went off half-
cocked, rules were established requiring majority or unani-
mous votes for all major actions, such as expenditures of more
than $10,000, production of new apparel designs and hiring of
additional employees.

With these guidelines established in principle, and each
party comforted by the fact that he or she would have both
freedom and built-in protection, all of the terms were put on
paper in the form of a Partnering Agreement. Signed and dated
by Stanley, Richard, and Diane, this critical document went beyond the initial contract that governed the company's legal
structure to set out just how the business would be run by the
key managers of the Good Looks assembly Line. In a matter of
months it proved to be the ideal catalyst and control mecha-
nism to get the company moving toward the growth plan management had projected for the business.

Evaluating the Partnership

The partnering process provides ample opportunity for both
personal and organizational learning, which is critical to continuously fine-tuning the assembly line and ultimately raising
the bar on knowledge worker productivity. In the enlightened
organization, learning comes from the individuals on the team

sharing ideas, pursuing challenges, and overcoming obstacles. This leads to individual and collective growth (as in the case of attorney Green and her firm Smythe, Smythe, & Smythe) and greater productivity.

To review what was gained from the partnering process, everyone involved in the collaboration should use the Learning Evaluation chart in Figure 9-3.

The evaluation part of the process should include participants in the Partnering Agreement. Tackle the evaluation this way:

- The learning evaluation commences with "what went well." Discuss whether or not key objectives were achieved. What were the consequences of your ability to achieve (or not achieve) the key objectives?
- Discuss the challenges you encountered. What steps did you take to anticipate and address these challenges? Were they effective? What changes would you make in the future?
- Finally, make a note of your personal and/or organizational learning that is directly attributable to the partnering experience. Capture thoughts and ideas for next time. Review these thoughts before commencing new projects. This will help you benefit from the wisdom you have gained.

Retain your Partnering Agreements for staff reviews and evaluations. And bear this in mind: An assembly line is a form of partnership. For it to function at peak performance, the partners must work as a team.

In an interesting and productive use of the partnering agreements, the founder/chairman of a chain of children's clothing shops hired a consultant to analyze the current state of her business. The results proved to be unsettling. The analysis revealed that the business was a chain in concept only; in practice, it functioned like a series of disconnected stores, run by managers who viewed their shops as private domains. Although the assembly line was far-flung, covering retail sites in six states, it had to work effectively if the business was to har-

Figure 9-3. Partnering agreement evaluation.

Learning Evaluation	
What went well:	Consequences:
Challenges:	Consequences / Solutions:

Learning	
Organizational:	Personal:

Notes:

ness the synergies that would, and could, lead to sustained growth.

In pursuit of this goal, the chairman sought a device that would link the stores into a cohesive, functional entity. Yes, the store managers would retain the authority to make localized purchasing and merchandising decisions, but they would recognize, and act on, the need to work as a team toward the achievement of broader corporate goals.

With this in mind, the chairman introduced partnering agreements into the management process and required all the store managers to sign them, both as a pledge of their commitment to work together, and to delineate all their responsibilities to each other, to various management committees, and to the business as a whole. This process—involving more than a dozen meetings to negotiate the responsibilities and implications of partnering—has had a powerful impact on the company, transforming the retail chain into a tightly knit business with a single mission. Today, when a store manager faces a daunting problem with employees, local competitors, or any of the complications that can make life difficult, an S-O-S e-mail system is in place that alerts the other managers to the problem. If a peer has experience in addressing the issue, arrangements are made for an in-person visit or conference call to facilitate a joint approach to the problem.

Clearly, with effective partnering, $2 + 2 = 5$.

Learning Review

Read through the learning review below and check those items that have particular relevance for you and/or your team. Once you have completed this, circle the *one item* that you feel has been a personal learning breakthrough, and discuss its significance with the other participants in the project.

☐ All knowledge workers must have a solid commitment to their work if it is to be truly valuable and meaningful, and be capable of adapting to a changing business environment. Put simply, they must take ownership of what they do.

☐ Ownership, responsibility, and accountability (ORA) are best achieved through a partnering process that forges an alliance between all participants in the work.

☐ The Partnering Agreement form is a tool for guiding teams through the productivity partnering process.

☐ An evaluation of the productivity partnership, including the consequences of what went well and what didn't, is vital for effective personal and organizational learning. This too is critical for responding to a changing environment and, in turn, achieving maximum productivity in even the most demanding business conditions.

LEARNING TRANSFER

Write a brief statement encapsulating your strengths and weaknesses as identified during your work in this chapter.

_____

_____

_____

_____

_____

10

The Power of Persuasion: Influencing While Maintaining Interpersonal Relationships

"Physical strength can never permanently withstand the impact of spiritual force."

—Franklin D. Roosevelt

Did you ever think that assembly lines, productivity, and astronomy have anything in common? Well, they do.

Astrophysicists have long been puzzled by a galactic mystery: Why galaxies weigh more than the sum of their visible parts. To solve this problem of so-called missing mass, the scientists have concocted theories about mysterious "dark matter" and "weakly interacting massive particles," known as W.I.M.P.S. Huge clouds of these W.I.M.P.S. supposedly make up the missing mass.

Interestingly, many companies suffer from a similar phenomenon. Their "missing mass" is evident in the form of "weakly interdependent management people." These W.I.M.P.S. work so ineffectively with others that their presence has little or no impact on the assembly line that produces the company's products and services.

This is unacceptable in today's prevailing business structures. Flattening of the hierarchy, along with the increasing emphasis on interdependence, requires that virtually every worker play a role in influencing others to serve the company's strategic purpose. Put simply, spontaneous leadership is required to solve problems and meet customer expectations.

This leads to a key point: By developing strategic influencing skills, you can become far more effective in the interdependent business environment.

That is precisely what this component of the assembly line (and this chapter) is designed to help you do. The first step is to determine how persuasive you are. You will do so by assessing your personal *influencing style,* and examining when it is most appropriately used.

Personal Exercise

Turn your attention to the Influencing Style Questionnaire, developed by Dr. Peter Honey, in Figure 10-1. As you see, there are forty statements describing different tendencies. Simply indicate in the box beside each statement how often you display each type of behavior. Use a 1 to 5 grading system, where 1 is "almost never" and 5 is "almost always."

Before scoring the questionnaire, let's take a look at the three kinds of influencing styles. Like everyone else, you find yourself in situations where you want to (1) influence others to get a decision to go your way, (2) change opinions or attitudes, or (3) persuade someone to take a course of action. The approach you select to achieve any of these "influencing" goals depends on the prevailing circumstances. Because there is no magic formula, you must pick and mix influencing styles as circumstances dictate.

Think of this as another dimension of situational awareness, and be aware that it is something you can learn. Being effective at situational awareness requires that you become

(text continues on page 112)

Figure 10-1. Influencing style questionnaire.

▼▼▼

Here are forty statements describing different tendencies. Simply indicate, as honestly as you can in the box beside each statement, how rarely or often you display each tendency. Please use the following "marking" system:

1. *Almost never/very seldom*
2. *Seldom*
3. *Occasionally*
4. *Frequently*
5. *Almost always/very frequently*

1. ☐ *I tend to hold strong views about most subjects.*

2. ☐ *I tend to offer alternatives to people and let them choose.*

3. ☐ *I am a friendly person and establish a good rapport with others.*

4. ☐ *Once I've reached a decision, I tend to stick to it.*

5. ☐ *When people oppose my views, I tend to question them to understand why.*

6. ☐ *I tend to ask other people for their views.*

7. ☐ *When someone says something I don't agree with, I don't hesitate to tell them so.*

8. ☐ *I seek common understanding prior to making decisions.*

9. ☐ *I tend to have to explain things to people.*

10. ☐ *I tend to interrupt other people.*

11. ☐ *I tend to modify my opinion after listening to other people's points of view.*

12. ☐ *When something goes wrong, I tend to determine who was to blame.*

13. ☐ *I use humor to give perspective to a situation, even when under tension.*

▲▲▲

(continues)

Figure 10-1   (Continued.)

▼▼▼

1. *Almost never/very seldom*
2. *Seldom*
3. *Occasionally*
4. *Frequently*
5. *Almost always/very frequently*

14. ☐ *I find it difficult to suffer fools gladly.*

15. ☐ *I tend to ask people lots of questions.*

16. ☐ *I tend to trust other people to perform well.*

17. ☐ *When things aren't progressing well, I take over, push ahead, and get the job done.*

18. ☐ *I tend to put cut-and-dried proposals to people.*

19. ☐ *I tend to talk more than I listen.*

20. ☐ *I tend to solicit the support of others.*

21. ☐ *I tend to override opposition to my views.*

22. ☐ *I pay careful attention to detail and double check all I can to correct errors.*

23. ☐ *I tend to aim for consensus decisions.*

24. ☐ *I put my ideas forward strongly.*

25. ☐ *I provide others with as much information as I think they need.*

26. ☐ *When persuading, I tend to concentrate on the benefits of a particular course of action.*

27. ☐ *I tend to criticize other people's actions.*

28. ☐ *I tend to avoid getting involved in conflict situations.*

▲▲▲

▼▼▼

1.　Almost never/very seldom
2.　Seldom
3.　Occasionally
4.　Frequently
5.　Almost always/very frequently

29. ☐ I tend to be forceful and dynamic.

30. ☐ I map out alternatives and help other people to decide on the best course of action.

31. ☐ I listen carefully to what others have to say.

32. ☐ When bad news has to be broken, I don't shirk from telling people in a straightforward way.

33. ☐ I continually check to see that people are doing things the way I want them done.

34. ☐ When something goes wrong, I tend to determine why mistakes occurred in order to prevent a recurrence.

35. ☐ I tend to be open-minded and base my decisions upon the thinking of the majority.

36. ☐ I tend to give people advice in an "If I were you, I'd do so and so" manner.

37. ☐ I openly communicate the whys and wherefores of a situation.

38. ☐ I tend to develop other people's ideas.

39. ☐ I tend to tell people what needs to be done.

40. ☐ I go out of my way to give encouragement to others.

▲▲▲

adept at choosing, and using, the appropriate influencing style for each set of circumstances.

Major styles include:

Directive:	"I decide what needs to be done and I tell the person/group what to do and how to do it."
Consultative:	"I ask the person/group for ideas, and then I decide what needs to be done."
Collaborative:	"I ask the person/group for ideas, and together we agree on what needs to be done."

As an effective manager or team player, your skill is knowing which of these styles to use on which occasion.

Now let's go back and score your questionnaire and decide on your style.

Scoring the Questionnaire

Look at the Influencing Style Questionnaire Score Key in Figure 10-2. Enter your answers in the appropriate boxes. Total the answers in column A and column B.

Now let's interpret your scores, using the table in Figure 10-3. Note that the interpretation table measures only two of the styles, directive and collaborative. The consultative style will always fall in the middle of any questionnaire. If your scores fall between 50 and 64 points or directive (column A), and between 60 and 74 points for collaborative (column B), then you can interpret your dominant style as consultative.

Meetings

There is no more important forum for influencing people than meetings. These sessions are where employees and managers (participants on the invisible assembly line) discuss issues, de-

(text continues on page 115)

Figure 10-2. Influencing style questionnaire score key.

A		B	
1.	☐	2.	☐
4.		3.	
7.		5.	
9.		6.	
10.		8.	
12.		11.	
14.		13.	
17.		15.	
18.		16.	
19.		20.	
21.		23.	
22.		26.	
24.		28.	
25.		30.	
27.		31.	
29.		34.	
32.		35.	
33.		37.	
36.		38.	
39.		40.	

Total
Score

Total
Score

*Directive
Influencing
Style*

*Collaborative
Influencing
Style*

Figure 10-3. Influencing style questionnaire interpretation.

Both the Directive and Collaborative styles are effective and appropriate at different times. Judging when to use which style is, in itself, an important skill. Directive is an "*I'll tell you what to do*" style. Collaborative is a "*together we'll agree on what to do*" style.   Directive is, therefore, an "I" style, whereas Collaborative is a "*we*" style.

When completing the questionnaire, people tend to use lower ratings for the Directive items than for the Collaborative items. In order to compare like with like, therefore, the scores are weighted differently. Please write your scores in the appropriate box below to discover their significance.

Directive Influencing Style	Collaborative Influencing Style	Interpretation
80 - 100	90 - 100	Style used very frequently/almost always.
65 - 79	75 - 89	Style used frequently.
50 - 64 (mean 57)	60 - 74 (mean 67)	Style used occasionally.
34 - 49	44 - 59	Style seldom used.
20 - 33	20 - 43	Style used almost never/very seldom.

velop strategies, share ideas, and resolve disputes. This accomplished, the *real* work can proceed more effectively.

The problem is that for most managers, meetings start early on Monday morning and go on and on throughout the week. Studies reveal that CEOs spend seventeen hours per week in meetings, senior executives spend a day a week (that's a twenty-four hour day!), and middle management spends an average of eleven hours per week meeting, meeting, meeting.

Are all these meetings really necessary? The answer may surprise you. In a Priority Management's International Business Lifestyle Survey, 22 percent of senior management and 29 percent of middle management reported that the meetings they attend could be replaced by phone calls or memos! Clearly, a great many meetings are deemed to be wasteful.

The poor results such meetings produce waste your time, waste the company's time, and squander money.

Meeting Costs

Direct Costs	Indirect Costs	Time Costs
Salaries	Employee benefits	Preparation time
Travel	Work not done/missed	Meetings time
Facilities	Frustration	Meetings to
Materials	Low morale	discuss
		meetings

No one is saying that meetings can or should be dispensed with. However, they must be transformed into useful sessions that reinforce the connections between people and resources, and help to achieve corporate objectives. When this occurs, the pendulum swings the other way: The company's goals and your career are advanced.

This section of the chapter will teach you the skills and processes you need to be successful at running meetings. Here, knowledge of influencing styles will be vital. This is important because when properly managed, meetings can and do get results.

The ultimate reward for learning how to operate in meetings is being able to run them to your own liking! Run properly, meetings should progress through these key phases:

- Achieving focus
- Having the necessary resources available
- Capturing results and outcomes
- Building an evaluation system

The best-run meetings are designed in this results-oriented sequence. At this point, go through the four-phase sequence in anticipation of your next meeting.

The Meeting Planner Form
(See Figure 10-4)

Phase 1

Steps You Can Take

Headline the main issue or purpose of the meeting. This has the following effects:

- It encourages staying on the topic at hand.
- It avoids time-costly squandering.
- It ensures that everyone is in the same room for the same purpose.

When listing the specific results to be achieved, remember:

- Use action verbs designed to achieve a results focus (e.g., decide, choose, approve, complete). Also, make sure that the goal (information, discussion, action) is reflected in the wording.
- Zero in on those aspects of the broader issue to be discussed and completed in the meeting (choose team, set objectives, etc.).
- These result statements should guide the structure of the meeting, enabling the selection of the appropriate participants, material, process; guide the discussion within

the meeting; and provide a base for evaluating the meeting.

At this point, note the results you would like to achieve in a meeting you are planning or will be attending. Put your comments in writing and use them to guide your conduct during the session.

Let's stop for a moment and remember that many meetings have little or no value. Before holding or attending a meeting, ask yourself:

- Is the subject up for discussion really my issue?
- Do I need a group to help me resolve it?
- How else might this result be achieved? Other ways might be:
  —One-on-one with a supervisor, co-worker, or vendor
  —Phone call/facsimile/electronic mail
  —Memo
  —Decide on my own
  —Include in another meeting

In summary, Phase 1 has provided you with the specific results to achieve, in the order you want to achieve them. And it provides you with guidelines for eliminating those meetings that are unworthy of your attendance, and for accomplishing the same goals through other means.

Phase 2

Phase 2 focuses our attention on *how* we can achieve the results we have just listed. It asks the questions, "What resources will I require to bring about these results, with respect to both people and information?" and "What will it cost?"

First, we should rewrite the Phase I results in order of priority. This step is important because:

- It gives form to the agenda (i.e., we should develop objectives, then terms, then teams).
- It forces you to reexamine the proposed content of the meeting, once again asking the question, "Should this really be part of this meeting?"

- It allows you to choose the right people and match them to the appropriate item. This is essential because it forces you to examine each result statement separately and to select people who can bring applicable skills or knowledge to bear on the issues.
- It ensures that each person attending is really instrumental for achieving the meeting result.

Plan Your Time Resources

- Review each result statement and estimate the time in minutes that should be required to complete the item.
- Place a time limit on each result to avoid undue length. Time limits stimulate an action orientation.
- Review estimates to see if all items fit sensibly into a single meeting.

With your next meeting in mind, set the date, start and end times, and location:

- Choose a date that fits the urgency of the issue and the availability of the resources.
- Add up the time required, allowing for introduction, conclusion, and evaluation, and select start and end times that allow for the completion of the meeting results.
- Select a time that is likely to avoid (1) lethargy (just after lunch), (2) delayed start (Monday 8:00 a.m.) or (3) distraction (Friday, 3:00 p.m.).
- Select a location appropriate to the purpose.

Determine the need for facilities, equipment, and special arrangements:

- Ensure that someone has accepted responsibility for all facilities, equipment, and other special arrangements.
- Note any special tasks and who will perform them.
- Contact participants to let them know what's expected of them.
- Arrange for a meeting facilitator, if necessary. This is

generally advisable when there is likely to be contention among the participants or when technical issues require explanation by an expert.
- Ensure that premeeting material is properly distributed. This helps to answer questions and raise critical issues that must be addressed at the outset.

Phases 1 and 2 will make significant contributions to your meetings—they will get you results and save you money.

Now let's move to Phase 3, the agenda that captures results and outcomes.

Phase 3

The agenda for a meeting can be created using the Agenda/Outcome page of the Meeting Planner (Figure 10-4).

On the top line, repeat the Issue/Purpose statement. Also, identify the chairperson or contact person for the meeting. This is important, as this person serves as the information source for what's needed, venue, and details. Enter the date, the start and end times, and the location.

Now construct the meeting agenda by rewriting the results statements (once again using action verbs). Use this sequence:

- Identify the introduction main subject and evaluation items.
- Identify the time of each item.
- Identify the result statement.
- Indicate the type of activity (using codes—INF for information, DIS for discussion, and ACT for action).

Other guidelines for creating the agenda:

- Keep the meeting to 1½ hours if possible.
- Put creative items at the beginning of an agenda.
- Start on a uniting theme. (This encourages buy-in from the participants.)
- End on a uniting theme. (This reinforces buy-in.)
- Once the meeting is complete, evaluate it in writing.

(text continues on page 122)

Figure 10-4. Meeting planner—agenda/outcomes.

Meeting (*Issue/Purpose*):

Specific Results To Be Achieved

Priority B A	By the time we leave this meeting we should have:	Meeting Test (Go/No Go)

To Achieve These Results I Will Need

Result By Priority	These people:	This information/material:	Reference	Time Required

Date: *Start time:*   *End time:*   *Location:*

Facilities/Equipment/Special Arrangements

Facilities/Equipment/Special Arrangements	Costs Est.	Act.	Ref.	Responsibility
Facilities & Equipment Costs				
Participant Costs				Plan Agenda Overleaf
Total Meeting Costs				

Meeting (Issue/Purpose):					☐ Chairperson: ☐ Contact:				
Date:		Start time:	End time:		Location:				
Item No.	Time	Agenda	Type	Decision/Action Summary		Ref	Priority	Who Account.	By/When

Meeting Evaluation

What went well	Problems to Overcome	Solutions

Attendees:

Apologies:

Next Meeting Date:	Start Time:	End Time:	Location:	On a scale of 1-10 this meeting was a	☐

After the meeting, distribute the minutes to all attendees, absentees, and other relevant people as soon as possible, preferably within one day. This provides a reminder to take the appropriate courses of action after the event. This is part of the process of planning, doing, evaluating. (Always include notes from the oral evaluation.)

Evaluating Meetings

If you implement the process approach to meetings that we have outlined, each session will increase in value and results by incorporating the improvements and suggestions from previous sessions. Be sure to record both the positive and negative aspects of the process and stress the importance of seeking solutions to problems you encounter. Also rate the meeting in terms of accomplishments and value. To reinforce the assembly line's collaborative approach, this should be done by the group, using a scale of 1 (lowest rating) to 10 (highest rating).

Learning to manage meetings and participate in them more effectively will have a positive impact on your career (which is based, in part, on your ability to influence people) as well as on your company (which must foster interdependence among employees, managers, and vendors). Not only will the time spent in meetings be cut dramatically, but meetings will become powerful management tools to motivate people and make things happen. The time invested in planning meetings is typically measured in hours, but the return will be measured in increased productivity and profitability.

Meeting Process Benefits

- Meetings are more effective, with a bias for action.
- Wasted time is reduced.
- You and your organization save money.
- Your meetings stay focused.
- Group memory greatly improves.
- Meetings are motivators.

Real-World Close-Up

A key benefit of engaging in a meeting process—as opposed to spontaneous sessions that lack planning, monitoring, and follow-up—is that the process facilitates benchmarking, enabling the company and its employees to determine what works and what simply wastes time in the plethora of meetings.

This was precisely the scenario at a San Jose, California–based computer products company, which we'll call Alpha Omega, that experienced explosive growth over a ten-year period. As hundreds of employees were hired to meet escalating demand, and new departments and subdepartments were formed continuously, meetings were essential for linking values and vision, mapping and implementing strategy, and simply making sure that everyone was moving in the same direction on the full scope of corporate projects.

But as senior management discovered, there can be too much of a good thing. Midway through the tenth anniversary of the company's founding—a year of 22 percent and 27 percent growth in revenues and employees, respectively—Alpha Omega began to resemble a mini-bureaucracy. Meetings loomed as a key problem. Once a critical part of the growth management process, they had become a narcotic and a crutch, used by managers and employees to justify their actions and "cover their bases" rather than to share ideas and gain consensus. In this environment, the company approached a state of internal paralysis, with staff and supervisors unwilling to accept responsibility and/or make decisions single-handedly (even in cases where they were clearly authorized to do so). The buck stopped at no one's desk. All responsibility was laid at the door of committees, and every action had become a product of compromise.

Recognizing that the company was strangling from within, and was thus in danger of forfeiting the great gains it had made in the marketplace, the CEO demanded that all meetings be charted, noting the purpose of the sessions, duration, participants, and outcome. After reviewing this documentation over a two-month period, he confirmed his worst suspicions: Alpha Omega held too many meetings. It was squandering valuable time in the pursuit of bureaucratic goals that were suffocating the company.

Acting decisively (something her managers and employees were having great trouble doing), the CEO announced guidelines for an Alpha Omega meeting process designed to break the logjam that was threatening the business while at the same time preserving the best qualities of effective meetings, specifically providing guidance and facilitation for a well-oiled assembly line.

Effective immediately, Alpha Omega's meetings would have to have these features:

- At least one manager must authorize the meeting in writing, briefly stating the purpose and desired outcome.
- Meetings are to last no longer than thirty minutes.
- Only people with a genuine "need to know" may attend.
- The manager authorizing the meeting must play an active role in follow-up, making certain that plans and strategies resulting from the meeting are implemented.
- Meetings that fail to produce substantive benefits are to be identified as time wasters. Where this applies to a category of meeting (e.g., Friday afternoon technical department meetings), the sessions are to be scuttled or restructured in the continuous effort to achieve a greater level of measurable benefits.

At Alpha Omega—and other equally enlightened companies—the goal is to make the meeting process enhance, rather than detract from, the proper functioning of the assembly line.

Learning Review

Read through the learning review below and check the items that have particular relevance for you and/or your team. Once you have completed this, circle the *one item* that you feel has been a learning breakthrough, and discuss its significance with your fellow participants.

☐ Every job in the information era calls for a leadership role.

☐ Strategic influencing skills, along with rational persuasion, lead to greater effectiveness in an interdependent workplace.

☐ Three influencing styles are typically adopted—directive, consultative, and collaborative. All of them are appropriate, depending on the situation.

☐ Situational awareness is the ability to choose the appropriate influencing style for the occasion.

☐ Meetings are often the forum for influencing and for gaining direction for the assembly line.

☐ Meetings are like all work—a process. To be most effective, the process must be controlled.

LEARNING TRANSFER

Write a brief statement encapsulating your strengths and weaknesses as identified during your work in this chapter.

_____

_____

_____

_____

_____

_____

11

The Continuous Improvement Process

"Knowledge is the only instrument of production that is not subject to diminishing returns."

—J. M. Clark, *Journal of Political Economy*, October 1927

The key ingredient that ensures the success of the knowledge-work assembly line, and your position on it, is *learning*. And even more than that, *continuous* learning. On Henry Ford's assembly line, employees were given instructions on simple tasks, and repeated those tasks for years. Today, the challenges—and the need to face up to them—change rapidly. Thus, continuous learning, is important.

Even an industrial giant with deep roots in the evolution of the traditional assembly line (Chevrolet) now recognizes that its white-collar employees must also work at a new level of interdependence, and that continuous learning is essential to this.

As a Chevrolet executive reveals, "We are pushing the corporation forward towards being a learning organization. We are working to change our culture so that our people view learning as more than an exercise, but as a competitive advantage."

To achieve this competitive advantage, Chevrolet has begun putting its field sales executives through the Priority Management Systems Process-Skills Analysis, identifying their strengths and weaknesses. The idea is to learn how to make these men and women more effective in working with dealers, consumers, and one another.

"The pace of change has been so dramatic, that the old ideas, the old knowledge, is no longer adequate." If Chevrolet is to remain competitive, it must make learning perpetual.

In fact, knowing *how* to learn is the most important business and personal skill, because it is the key to future success. Once you learn how to learn, you can achieve competency in all workplace skills.

This relates to the inescapable fact that knowledge acquisition, knowledge assimilation, and knowledge transfer are central to success in the interdependent, highly productive workplace (see Figure 11-1). Companies and individuals that put these three building blocks in place will have a matchless advantage in the marketplace. They will be able to provide the continuous improvements in quality and productivity that are required to meet the competitive standards of the information-age economy.

Once you know how to learn, this knowledge will serve as a recipe for continuous improvement and for helping others develop and improve. With this in mind, here's what you need to know about learning:

• Learning is not just knowing the answers (rote learning) or giving a conditioned response (like teaching a parrot to talk). It is a matter of increasing knowledge, skills, and perspective.

• Many believe that learning "just happens" as a consequence of living. Many people summarize this belief as "learning to cope." But learning to cope is a recipe for survival, whereas learning from experience is a recipe for continuous improvement.

• Learning is not automatic. It requires considerable effort, persistence, and support.

• "You can't teach an old dog new tricks" is a common misconception about the learning process. An old dog can still learn if there is a tension for change. Indeed, lifelong learning is the recipe for lifelong success.

Figure 11-1. Building the learning organization.

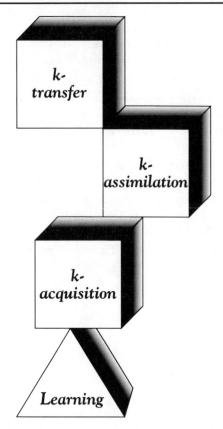

- Learning is not just for intellectuals—it is the lubricant of change and therefore involves us all. We cannot choose to ignore it.

- Many believe that we all learn the same way. This is not so! Evidence suggests that people develop significantly different ways of learning. Some learn best by doing, some by watching, some by understanding the theory and principles, and some by utilizing "how-to" tips or techniques. In other words, just as in influencing, there are learning style preferences.

- Finally, some believe that learning isn't necessary when things are going well. Not so. Learning from success is just as valid and useful a process as learning from mistakes.

The Learning Cycle

Dr. Peter Honey has discovered that learning from experience is a process that can be broken down into component parts. To do so, imagine a circle with four stages at the four points of the compass (see Figure 11-2).

Stage 1: Having an Experience

Learning from experience is greatly enhanced when the everyday things that happen to us are supplemented by the extra experiences we create. Suppose, for example, you attend a weekly management meeting that tends to be deadly dull. You could decide to view it as a learning opportunity and start to experiment with different ways of participating in or running the meeting. In the process, you will be turning an everyday event into a learning experience that is central to continuous improvement. When the time comes to act on this experience you will be in a position to advance personal and corporate interests.

Figure 11-2. The "learning from experience" cycle.

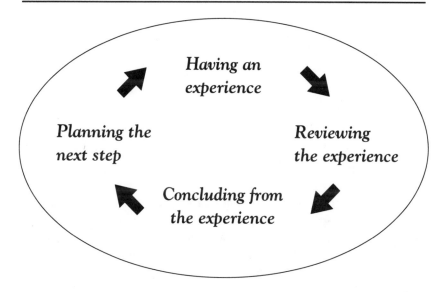

Stage 2: Reviewing the Experience

If you are to learn from an experience, it is vital that you review what happened during it. In the dull management meeting, you might experiment by having different people take the chair for different agenda items. Your review might focus on the differences you observed between the way the best and worst chairpersons undertook the task.

Stage 3: Concluding from the Experience

Concluding involves scanning the experience for observations, answers, or lessons learned. It helps if the conclusions are specific. After the management meeting, you might conclude that the best chairperson:

- Kept to the agenda.
- Clarified the objective of the agenda discussion.
- Actively sought other people's ideas.
- Summarized the group's thinking at frequent intervals.
- Finished with an evaluation process.

This is valuable input for improving future meetings and raising the productivity levels attributable to them—and ultimately raising the productivity of the company's ongoing procedures and processes.

Stage 4: Planning the Next Step

Planning involves translating some of the conclusions of your learning experience into actions. An example might be to spend ten minutes at the start of the next meeting discussing your conclusions about the best chairperson and working out a plan for helping those who had the most difficulty with that person's style or approach. The idea is to put the best person in place and create an environment that helps that person achieve maximum effectivensss.

Learning as a Continuous Process

All of the stages in the process of learning from experience are dependent on one another. No one stage makes sense, or is particularly useful, in isolation from the others.

You can start anywhere in the cycle because each stage feeds into the next. A person could, for example, start at Stage 2 by acquiring information and pondering it before reaching conclusions in Stage 3, and deciding how to apply them in Stage 4. On the other hand, another person could start at Stage 4 (see Figure 11-3) with a technique he or she plans to incorporate into his or her modus operandi. The technique would then be used at Stage 1 in the cycle. The person would then review how the technique worked out in Stage 2, reach conclusions concerning it in Stage 3, and modify it in the light of the experience for Stage 4.

This continuous, repetitive process is fundamental to effective personal and group learning. Consider the real-world case of a prominent apparel design and manufacturing firm that produced a creative new line of clothing that management believed would generate exceptional sales and profits. Although the line was attractive and trend-setting, it suffered from a fatal flaw: It was priced too high for its target market. As a result, the venture was a costly flop.

Although a number of factors contributed to this disaster, the real killer was that management failed to recognize the invisible assembly line that connects production with marketing. Put simply, no one bothered to ask the salespeople if the line would sell—until it was too late. That's the bad news. The good news is that the company learned from its mistake, identifying the assembly line and engineering it so that the marketing department would have to provide input (based on its knowledge and experience) at the earliest stage of new product development.

Caveats in Learning

Dr. Honey has found that most people develop preferences for certain stages of the learning cycle. This can lead to a distortion

Figure 11-3. Learning log (example).

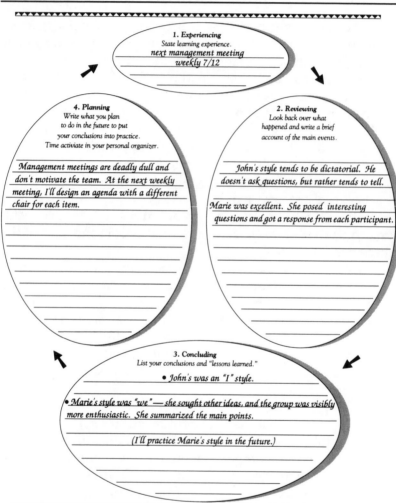

of the learning process because greater emphasis is placed on these stages, to the detriment of others. Here are some typical examples:

• *Preferences for experiencing.* Some people develop an addiction to activities to such an extent that they cannot sit still but have to rush around constantly. This results in plenty of experiences and the assumption that having experiences is synonymous with learning from them.

• *Preferences for reviewing.* Some people postpone reaching conclusions for as long as possible while they gather more and more data. This results in an "analysis to paralysis" tendency, with plenty of pondering but little action. In the example of the apparel firm, a line must be produced for each season. Input must be given, but in a way that allows action (production of the line) to be taken in a narrow time frame.

• *Preferences for "concluding."* People have a compulsion to reach an answer quickly. This results in a tendency to jump to conclusions by circumventing the review stage, where uncertainty and ambiguity are higher. Sometimes, conclusions— even if they are the wrong ones—are comforting things to have. But they are often premature.

Application Exercise: The Learning Log™

In Figure 11-4, you will find two blank Learning Logs™. They have been designed to help you and your team implement the learning cycle in your everyday activities. As you tackle the Learning Logs, bear in mind that this activity can be carried out alone or in teams.

Real-World Close-Up

The tendency to sweep mistakes under the rug (which is deeply ingrained in many corporate cultures) is the greatest obstacle to continuous learning. This blatant act of self-indulgence enables management and employees to shirk responsibility for their errors and misjudgments. Rather than identifying *what* went wrong and *why* the failure occurred, the company (individually and collectively) fails to deal with the breakdown and to counsel and/or penalize those responsible

(text continues on page 136)

Figure 11-4. Learning logs (blank).

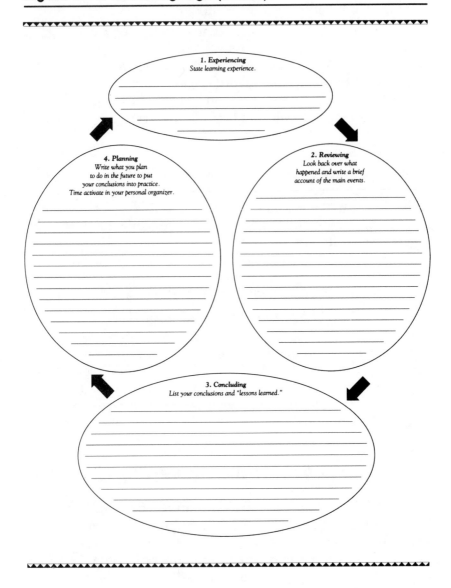

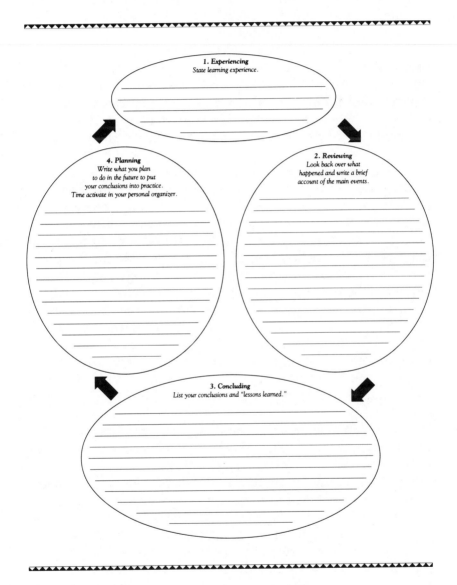

for it. Although this may protect sensitive egos and maintain an aura of well-being, it actually perpetuates and thus institutionalizes the flaws in the system.

To prevent this, the most enlightened companies—those committed to continuously reengineering the assembly line to achieve maximum productivity—relentlessly pursue errors and deficiencies, identifying them and communicating all they know about them to management and staff. Armed with this information, they seek ways to improve the way they do business.

For example, the executive committee of a Fortune 500 consumer products company is composed of the senior managers responsible for each of the company's lines of business. The committee meets every other Friday to review problems that have been identified by employees, customers, distributors, or other external constituencies. Those responsible for the problem, failure, or breakdown attend the meeting—not to be the target of criticism, but to explain what went wrong and why it occurred, so that management has the input it needs to develop corrective measures. Once the issues have been analyzed and the appropriate remedies established, the executive committee communicates its findings to all of the managers and staff. The idea is to share information so that everyone can play a role in the continuous learning (and continuous improvement) process.

This is somewhat similar to the approach taken by the National Transportation Safety Board in its never-ending quest to reduce the incidence of air travel accidents and increase the safety of air travel. Within hours after an accident, NTSB investigators are dispatched to the scene to explore the wreckage for any clues to the cause of the mishap. Whether it takes days, weeks, or months, investigators continue their probe until all the pieces of the puzzle fall into place. Through this painstaking process, the safety board has compiled an impressive record in reducing the frequency of air travel accidents. In essence, the NTSB has served as the catalyst for a continuous learning process, gathering critical data and sharing those data with the airline industry. The NTSB's managers are strict adherents to the learning cycle—always reviewing the "black box" tape (what actually happened) before making conclusions and passing on guidelines to the travel industry.

In all likelihood, your company has nothing to do with travel safety, and may not be making life-and-death decisions, but the methodologies used by this government agency can serve as a model for continuously improving your business and its profitability over the years.

Learning Review

Read through the learning review below and check those items that have particular relevance for you and/or your team. Once you have completed this, circle the *one item* that you feel has been a personal learning breakthrough, and discuss its significance with your coworkers.

☐ Learning to learn is a fundamental skill. By learning to learn, you can achieve competence in all other workplace skills.
☐ It is difficult to change if you don't know how to learn.
☐ The key steps in the learning cycle are:
  —Having an experience
  —Reviewing the experience
  —Concluding from the experience
  —Planning the next step
☐ Learning should be a continuous and iterative process.

LEARNING TRANSFER

Write a brief statement encapsulating your strengths and weaknesses as identified during your work in this chapter.

_____

_____

_____

_____

_____

12

The Values Gap

"The clock, not the steam engine, is the key machine of the industrial age."

—Lewis Mumford

Oscar Wilde once said that "work is the refuge of people who have nothing better to do." If that is true, a recent international survey we conducted would suggest that we are all becoming time-trapped refugees. The October 22, 1994 edition of *The Economist* noted the following:

- Factory workers are working longer hours now than at any time in the past half century.
- Executives and lawyers boast an average of eighty-hour weeks.
- Americans take two weeks of vacation a year, while even the Japanese are taking three, and the Germans six.

The Values Gap, an international survey conducted by Priority Management Systems, of time and value conflicts in the 1990s workplace, demonstrates that working smarter (as through a well-functioning assembly line) will give people the opportunity to achieve more balance between the business and personal components of their lives and add to their sense of fulfillment, well-being, and productivity.

Values, Balance, and Productivity

A new world economic structure based on knowledge is supplanting the old industrial society. Paralleling the rise of this "new economy" is a social revolution spearheaded by the re-emergence of personal ideals and values. As we moved into the 1990s, these issues rose rapidly to the top of the business agenda. Clearly, an understanding of how the values revolution is likely to affect the workplace is vital to business success in the twenty-first century.

Values are the personal beliefs we hold about things that are important to us. As we begin to adjust to the competitive realities of a new economy, the time-honored values of family and community are regaining their traditional place as guides and beacons for living within a moral and ethical framework. Our international survey found that people everywhere are paying more attention to their values and the way they live their lives, yet ever-increasing time constraints are forcing them to strike an uneasy balance among work, family, social, and community obligations.

Indeed, organizations and corporations are also recognizing the importance of aligning corporate and personal values. A workplace where employee and corporate values are in harmony is a productive one. Workers are happier, employee turnover and absenteeism drop, and productivity improves. Productivity is a function not only of how long people work, but also of how long they do not work. An ability to understand the importance of balancing values in business will be one of the most effective management skills in the workplace of the twenty-first century.

Methodology

The Values Gap survey is based on a questionnaire with sixty-two multiple choice questions, organized to illustrate social attitudes concerning the workplace, the family, time, and public issues such as volunteerism, the work ethic, and working with others.

One thousand middle- and upper-management employees from Australia, Belgium, Canada, Ireland, New Zealand, Portugal, Singapore, Spain, the United Kingdom, and the United States were surveyed, with a response rate of 87 percent. Over 90 percent of the respondents were between the ages of twenty and forty-nine; 67 percent were married, 20 percent single, and the remainder separated, divorced, or widowed. They represented a broad cross section of business interests, including the manufacturing, insurance, government, business service, and health care sectors, with annual incomes ranging from $20,000 to over $100,000.

Cluster analysis was used to organize respondents' fundamental values and lifestyle approaches and their concerns on a number of workplace issues. Four psychographic groups with consistent values and beliefs regarding these workplace issues are identifiable. The results have a 95 percent confidence level.

Value Groups:
Our Psychographic Segments

Four distinct psychographic segments emerge from the survey. Each is composed of people with similar values and attitudes toward various workplace issues, lifestyle approaches, and their use of time. We have called these groups interdependent humanists, compliant traditionalists, aggressive individualists, and mainstream conformists.

Interdependent Humanists (33 percent)

Typically trusting and displaying a sincere interest in others, the members of this group, more than any other, feel that part of their job is to offer emotional support to the people around them. These people are keenly interested in society and are the most active in volunteer work. Of all the psychographic groupings, they are the most likely to adhere to their own systems of personal values. They are the least respectful group with regard to seniority and authority, and the group most likely to take risks in both their personal and business affairs. While they feel that money is not all-important, 32 percent of the group earn more than $60,000 a year.

Compliant Traditionalists (27 percent)

Compliant traditionalists are most comfortable with time-honored opinions, doctrines, and practices and place a premium on higher education. They are the most deferential to seniority, the company, authority, and, of course, law and order, and typically volunteer less than any other group. An important subset of this group is the "new" compliant traditionalist. These are people in their twenties and early thirties who feel a strong affinity toward education and are concerned with both law and order and personal success. Fully 42 percent of all survey respondents under the age of twenty-nine are "new" traditionalists. This psychographic segment is the most optimistic about improving employee attitudes and the work ethic.

Aggressive Individualists (21 percent)

Aggressive individualists are independent-minded and success-oriented. They take responsibility for their own achievements and exhibit self-reliance, even denying the need for emotional support. They are less respectful of both authority and seniority than the conformists and traditionalists, but place a premium on the credentials of higher education. Surprisingly, they work the shortest hours of all the groups, yet feel that they have the least balance in their lives. Individualists may have had their heyday in the boom years of the 1980s; while they are still common, less than one in four people now fall into this segment of the population. The "bloom is off the boom" as adherents question the personal cost of an all-business lifestyle.

Mainstream Conformists (19 percent)

Generally disillusioned, this group represents the survivors of the downsized and reorganized workplace. Mainstream conformists are the smallest of these value groups. They have the least amount of control over their lives, typically work the longest hours (over nine hours daily), commute the farthest, and value money less than the other groups. They tend to be reactive, having to deal with developments brought about by others. Caught between the cost cutting of upper management and the frustration of overworked colleagues, mainstream conformists suffer high stress levels. Of the four segments, this group seems the farthest from gaining control over their work and personal lives. Their long days and long commutes leave them the least amount of time for family, friends, or themselves. Not surprisingly, these are the respondents who most want to spend more time at home.

Timelock

The Values Gap illustrates that people are working harder and longer to maintain their standard of living. Our respondents work an average of almost nine hours a day during the week and manage an additional hour of business work on weekends. All demographic sectors surveyed want to reduce their work commitment by at least an hour a day (see Figure 12-1).

Longer workdays have resulted in less time for other activities—less time for family, friends, community, spiritual reflection, and self. Gridlocked by overcrowded highways and streets and by prolonged commutes, the 1990s workers return home to find themselves time-locked by overscheduled evenings and weekends, by family demands, and by the nagging feeling that there should be some time to do nothing—to just unwind and relax.

The survey finds that gaining more time for family, social, and community pursuits is a vitally important lifestyle priority for respondents. Little wonder, since some 70 percent of the typical waking workday is taken up by work and the commute to and from the workplace. This leaves a meager 4½ hours per day to relate to spouses, children, parents, friends, and community, as well as to read, relax, and, of course, look after mind, body, and soul.

Figure 12.1 How we spend our discretionary day.

Sleep, meal preparation, and personal hygiene are combined to total the nondiscretionary time in the day. What is left is the discretionary day.

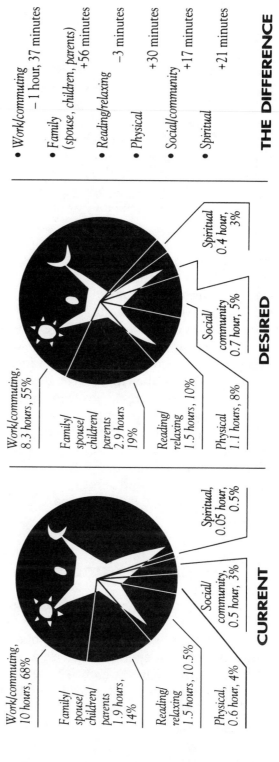

CURRENT

Work/commuting, 10 hours, 68%

Family/ spouse/ children/ parents 1.9 hours, 14%

Reading/ relaxing 1.5 hours, 10.5%

Physical, 0.6 hour, 4%

Social/ community, 0.5 hour, 3%

Spiritual, 0.05 hour, 0.5%

DESIRED

Work/commuting, 8.3 hours, 55%

Family/ spouse/ children/ parents 2.9 hours 19%

Reading/ relaxing 1.5 hours, 10%

Physical 1.1 hours, 8%

Social/ community 0.7 hour, 5%

Spiritual 0.4 hour, 3%

THE DIFFERENCE

- Work/commuting
  – 1 hour, 37 minutes
- Family
  (spouse, children, parents)
  +56 minutes
- Reading/relaxing
  –3 minutes
- Physical
  +30 minutes
- Social/community
  +17 minutes
- Spiritual
  +21 minutes

Along with the rise in demand for more family time come the concerns of living in an uncertain economy. The Values Gap shows that, overall, financial security is now the major concern of respondents, replacing the demand for more family time (except in Australia, where the family is still the number one priority). Also, 45 percent report being more concerned about money and material things than they were five years ago. Increasing financial concerns have made many less willing to question the operational and productivity demands of the new economy.

All groups want to reduce the daily time allotted to working and commuting by just over 1½ hours a day. Of that, they would like to work one hour and seventeen minutes less each day. Commuting still ranks as a major source of irritation, requiring on average an hour and a quarter a day. People everywhere would like to reduce their commute time by a third.

Women are increasingly time-locked by the demands of work, home, and family responsibilities. Accelerating time lock is the dual track that many women are now negotiating. For many, the career track has been joined by the "daughter track." Women respondents already spend almost three times as much of their day on caring for parents as do men. However, male respondents are spending slightly more time with their children and spouses than women respondents. Women have a shorter workday and tend to have a shorter commute than men, but spend more time preparing meals and getting ready for work.

The Shift to Family and Community

Overall, the survey respondents showed a desire to return to the values of past generations, and the family is at the center of that shift. Respondents report the need for one to two hours more each day to spend with family and friends and on community activities The difference between the current reality and the desired future creates a strong tension for change that workplace attitudes and values are only beginning to reflect (see Figure 12-2).

Figure 12-2. Tension for change reflected in workplace attitudes and values.

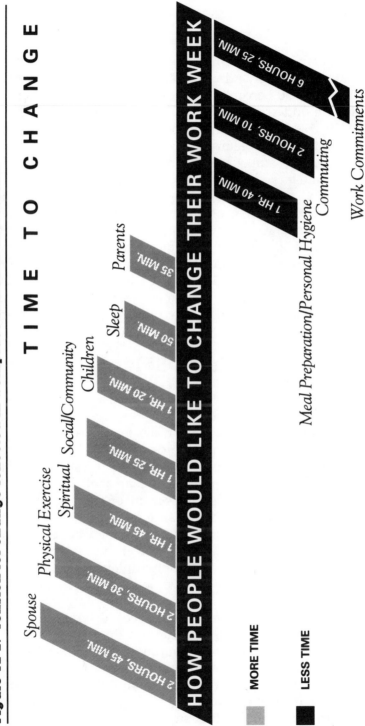

TIME TO CHANGE

HOW PEOPLE WOULD LIKE TO CHANGE THEIR WORK WEEK

Spouse — 2 HOURS, 45 MIN.

Physical Exercise — 2 HOURS, 30 MIN.

Spiritual — 1 HR, 45 MIN.

Social/Community — 1 HR, 25 MIN.

Children — 1 HR, 20 MIN.

Sleep — 50 MIN.

Parents — 35 MIN.

Meal Preparation/Personal Hygiene — 1 HR, 40 MIN.

Commuting — 2 HOURS, 10 MIN.

Work Commitments — 6 HOURS, 25 MIN.

MORE TIME

LESS TIME

This tension for change has been exacerbated by massive upheavals within organizations around the world. In every survey country, 50 percent of respondents report that their companies are undergoing major change most of the time. This results in two out of three respondents feeling constant uncertainty and ambiguity in the workplace.

Generally, our survey found that men and women are equally time-locked and that both genders are feeling the same stresses and strains of coping with the hectic and unrelenting pace of work. Women are more concerned than men about spending time with parents, on social/community activities, and on spiritual matters. They also place a higher priority on physical exercise. Men are more concerned about finding time for their spouses and children. Overall, women definitely feel more time-locked, stating that they need on average thirty minutes more per day than men to accomplish their personal goals.

Striking a Balance

Almost 85 percent of survey respondents are more concerned about leading a balanced life than they were five years ago. Only one in fifty feel that they always lead a balanced life, and 60 percent do not have a plan to close this gap and correct the imbalance. We found the situation to be worst in the United Kingdom, where 83 percent have no plan at all; it's best in Australia/New Zealand, where 50 percent of respondents have a strategy in place to close the balance gap.

One in two respondents see a declining work ethic. This is especially true of respondents who feel their companies to be unconcerned with whether or not employees lead a balanced life. More than half of those people believe the work ethic is getting worse.

Within these companies, employees also report increased employee turnover and little action on the issue of sexual harassment. Of the four psychographic groups, interdependent humanists view the work ethic with the most pessimism. The United Kingdom reports the highest improvement—54 percent of respondents feel the work ethic is improving. This contrasts with only 33 percent in other survey countries.

Half of American and Canadian respondents indicate that their vacations generally last less than seven days. The average person has just over two vacations per annum. Most Australians and New Zealanders take only two vacations a year. However, like the Europeans, 72 percent of them take vacations of two or more weeks at a time.

As work becomes more of a collective activity and the distinction between manager and managed blurs, the interdependent humanists are poised to prosper most in this democratic environment. Over 84 percent of this psychographic segment are willing to trust others until proven wrong, and they are the group most supportive of sexual equality at work. They also relish diversity in the workplace—almost 50 percent of this group seldomly or never allow racial characteristics to affect their personal or business relationships, and 97 percent of this group never allow color or race to enter into their value judgments of people.

This is in marked contrast to the aggressive individualists, who show tendencies toward color and racial bias, and to the mainstream conformists, who are less committed to sexual equality in the workplace than the other groups. The interdependent humanists seem also to be the group prospering most from their value systems—they make up almost half of all respondents earning over $80,000 per annum.

Organizations supporting balanced lifestyles for employees reap the benefits of improved worker morale and productivity. Respondents working in these companies and organizations reported more positive employee attitudes and an improved work ethic. They also report that potential value conflicts between themselves and the organization are reduced. Almost 50 percent of respondents from these companies have the key to remove the time lock—a plan to strike a balance between their professional and personal lives.

Conclusions

Whether values are viewed as benchmarks for the way we live or the way organizations function, their role in society and how widely they are misunderstood have become major impediments to individual happiness and corporate productivity. Both employers and employees need to recognize that the values gap will have to be bridged and that managing values in the workplace will be a crucial ingredient of business success during the 1990s and into the twenty-first century. A values revolution needs to occur in order for business to thrive, not merely survive, in these transformational times.

Our four psychographic groups—the interdependent humanists, the compliant traditionalists, the aggressive individualists, and the mainstream conformists—all voiced one overriding concern: to create a balance between home and work. The major victim of the values gap is without doubt the family, which has borne the assault of the changeover from the mass-production economy to the new economy. The pace at home now rivals the pace at the office. Children, spouses, and parents are as tightly scheduled as the most sophisticated business meeting. "Combination women," juggling home, work, children, and parents, are increasingly under pressure and display the greatest amount of stress.

People of all types are keenly aware that their lives are unbalanced and that they should do something to change this—they just haven't worked out what they should do. Evidence suggests that those who have surfaced and understand their values can change things for the better.

In order to close the values gap and achieve a balanced lifestyle, two factors need to be addressed. First, we need to live smarter, and second, we are going to have to work smarter. The former will result in more stability and balance in our lives and a happier home life, but it will arrive on the heels of working smarter, not before.

Working smarter—not longer or harder—will increase our productivity in a competitive world economy and allow us to go home and live smarter. Here's how.

Working Smarter

Surface and review your organization's values on a regular basis, and align them with your personal values.

Recognize that clarified values will contribute to a clear mission for the organization. Clarification of values and mission can dramatically increase the productivity of a workforce.

Resolve to reduce nonproductive tasks. Obliterate before you automate. Avoiding makework projects and concentrating on the task at hand will increase productivity while freeing up time for other activities.

Remember that if work can't be measured, you may not be able to manage it. Define the quantity and quality of the work to be accomplished, and make the employees, or your colleagues, partners in the definition.

Recognize employee needs for financial security, but also remember that boosting the productivity of the workplace will occur mainly through providing meaningful challenges and responsibility. These challenges must be closely aligned with personal values.

Living Smarter

Surface and review your personal values on a regular basis. Discuss them with your spouse, family, and friends. Write them down—even set priorities on the ones that are most important to you.

Once you have reviewed them, use your values to set goals and give priority to the ones that give your life direction and purpose.

Become a lifelong learner. You may have to obtain additional education and training to achieve your goals.

If the 1980s were defined by "more," make the 1990s the decade of "less." Rampant consumerism may trap you in a cycle of work–spend–work.

Make sure your schedule includes time for family, friends, community, and other key expressions of your values. Regrets later in life usually focus on misspent time—especially time not spent with children or parents. Do something about it now! Practice priority management every single day—don't try to accomplish everything. Recognize the difference between important and urgent.

Understand the values of those around you, both at home and at work. If these are dissonant with your own values, decide how you can change the situation. Express what you believe in and why. Others may follow.

Don't become a playaholic—a person who schedules every minute, including leisure time. Remember that downtime should have restorative and recuperative as well as recreational benefits. Plan to just do nothing occasionally.

In an increasingly competitive world, raising the productivity of the workforce is paramount. The best way to achieve this is to focus on and improve the health, morale, and personal productivity of employees by recognizing the importance of their personal values in the workplace and helping them to work smarter. The spinoff benefit for workers and management is that working smarter also allows people to live smarter.

The march of human progress has been toward greater interdependence—interdependence of villages, towns, states, and even entire continents. As technology and globalization transform the workplace, it is clear that command and control bureaucracies can no longer keep pace with massive change. No one person, nor indeed a single organization, can possess and process all the knowledge and technology necessary to remain competitive—hence the move to interdependent structures. This is changing the way we work.

At the same time, the combination of a more competitive global economy and an interdependent workplace has created a gap between personal and corporate values that must be closed. People today are working longer and harder, and many are aware of a noticeable imbalance in their lives. Our research highlights the values gap as the predominant issue in the workplace today.

Values are anchors that stop us from drifting away, especially during turbulent times. It is essential that organizations and individuals take time to surface their values and ensure that their activities reflect their ideals. Only then can we begin to select priorities, cut back, and slow down. The payoff will be a shift toward a future that holds the promise of a more purposeful and fulfilling life.

Epilogue

"Knowledge is power."

—Thomas Hobbes, *Leviathan*

As we have discovered, an invisible assembly line composed of eight knowledge work processes is critical for achieving a high level of individual and corporate performance.

On the front lines, in the workplace, these eight processes must be implemented by knowledge workers. This brings us to what we refer to as the core competencies, defined as "the capabilities of team members to perform the essential work processes."

The core competencies can be portrayed in a competency map.

There are four major performance areas (see Figure E-1). The first two are self-management and working with others. We see here the dichotomy between dependence and interdependence. The third and fourth competencies are asset/resource management and task/activity management.

Tensions among the four areas always exist. For example, there is tension between independence and interdependence (i.e., self and others), and between tasks and activities and the available resources (time, money, equipment, etc.). The ability to manage these tensions is the art of effectiveness. The core competencies serve as indicators of your ability to perform in these various situations. To assess your strengths and weaknesses, and in the process to develop benchmarks for raising the bar on personal and companywide performance, we have developed an effectiveness questionnaire designed in two parts

Figure E-1. The four major areas of the competency map.

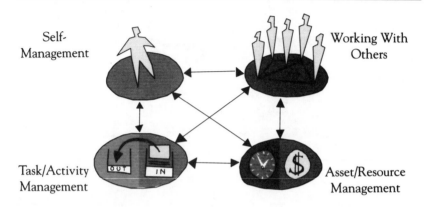

Self-
Management

Working With
Others

Task/Activity
Management

Asset/Resource
Management

to assure both *personal effectiveness* and *organizational effective-ness*. You will find this questionnaire in Figure E-2. Detach your completed answer sheet and send to Priority Management Systems, Inc., 500 108th Avenue, Bellevue, Washington 98004, and you will receive an analysis of your personal and collective core competencies, including how you compare to others. (Only original answer sheets from this book can be accepted.)

As you review the findings, bear in mind that benchmarking is a competitive technique for both organizations and individuals. It is a means for comparing your performance to that of others, and it serves as a jumping-off point for progress and improvement. In this way, it serves as a catalyst for the company to increase both profitability and market share and for the employees to make dramatic improvements in self-esteem, effectiveness, and success.

The true value of benchmarking is that it spurs companies and individuals to pursue a plan of action leading to higher performance levels. This can be done only by establishing new functional goals, implementing specific actions and behaviors, and finally measuring and monitoring your progress. The process begins with benchmarking, but the real value is in the process that leads to your personal improvement.

Now that you have read this book and are about to implement its strategies and techniques, be aware that you are embarking on a learning experience—a transformation that will change the way you peform as a knowledge worker and, in turn, that will change the way your company pursues its goals and objectives, competes in the marketplace, and produces products and services.

Before you set off on this journey of learning and self-improvement, let's remember precisely what you are seeking to accomplish. The major objectives are to:

- Succeed in the so-called SWAT functions of knowledge work.
  S Self-management
  W Working with others
  A Asset/resource management
  T Task management
- To differentiate between processes of production and the tools of production in knowledge work.
- To gain personal insight into your current level of performance.
- To develop your strategic thinking capabilities. As part of this, you will learn how to fuse values and vision into achievable strategies, and how to build in future considerations when setting broad-scale objectives for yourself and your team.
- To develop sound decision-making criteria for the allocation of resources.
- To apply priority management skills that enable you to distinguish the urgent from the routine and to identify value-added activities as opposed to those that simply complicate corporate processes.
- To develop a performance measurement system through an understanding of the quality/quantity balance of work.
- To build productivity partnerships between the key assembly line collaborators in each phase or component of work, and to establish ownership, responsibility, and accountability for all activities.

(text continues on page 165)

Figure E-2. The Effectiveness Questionnaire: Process-Skills Analysis™.

THE EFFECTIVENESS QUESTIONNAIRE:

PROCESS-SKILLS ANALYSIS™

Process-Skills Analysis™, the diagnostic component of the **PQ-I** *Development Process, is a measurement technique of both personal and organizational effectiveness.*

The resulting data facilitate reliable benchmarking in key developmental areas and act as a platform for improved **PQ-I** *— productivity, quality, and interdependence.*

▲▼

ABOUT
THE EFFECTIVENESS
QUESTIONNAIRE

This questionnaire is designed to establish your overall effectiveness at work. It is in two parts: **Part One** *asks questions about you as an individual, and* **Part Two** *asks questions designed to establish your views about your current organization.*

There are three possible answers to each question: a, b, or c. When you have decided which answer is truest for you, clearly mark the appropriate circle on the answer sheet provided. **Do not mark the questionnaire itself;** *all your answers should be recorded on the answer sheet. If more than one statement in an item applies, mark the* **ONE** *most typical of you or your organization, however marginal the difference.*

Please answer as honestly as possible what is true for you. Do not mark what you hope is the right thing to say because this will not give you a meaningful result.

Thank you.

▲▼

(continues)

Figure E-2   (Continued.)

▲▲

Part One

Remember to mark ONE circle ON THE ANSWER SHEET PROVIDED.

Example:
  a) ○

  b) ●

  c) ○

Please DO NOT make any marks on the questionnaire itself.

(1) *In conversations where morals or ethics are involved, I find myself*
   a) *considerably influenced by other people's arguments and points of view.*
   b) *partially influenced by other people.*
   c) *guided by strong basic beliefs about what is right and what is wrong.*

(2) *I am able to show how my actions and decisions relate to an overall strategy / my longer-term goals*
   a) *sometimes.*
   b) *most of the time.*
   c) *if I'm pushed.*

(3) *I believe it is of paramount importance to*
   a) *achieve what I can with the resources I have.*
   b) *tailor my objectives to the resources available.*
   c) *secure adequate resources in order to achieve my objectives.*

(4) *I tend to*
   a) *focus on things that are required urgently.*
   b) *focus on the things that are important.*
   c) *do both.*

(5) *My "bottom line" position is that*
   a) *quality is more important than quantity.*
   b) *quantity is more important than quality.*
   c) *both are equally important.*

(6) *When things haven't gone well, I tend to*
   a) *accept responsibility — even though some factors were outside my control.*
   b) *show how factors outside my control were the cause.*
   c) *accept responsibility but emphasize the influence of factors outside my control.*

(7) *More often than not I use*
   a) *a directive style: "This is what I've decided to do."*
   b) *a consultative style: "I'd like your ideas, then I'll decide."*
   c) *a collaborative style: "Let's decide together."*

(8) *I'm the sort of person who*
   a) *questions the way things are done.*
   b) *waits for others to ask the questions.*
   c) *accepts the status quo.*

(9) *When something happens that challenges my deep-seated beliefs, I tend to*
   a) *regard my beliefs as "non-negotiable" fixtures.*
   b) *question the continued validity of those beliefs.*
   c) *seek a compromise.*

(10) *When I have an urgent problem to solve, I*
   a) *move fast and decisively.*
   b) *do a thorough diagnosis by gathering relevant data.*
   c) *do something to put the situation "on hold" and give me some thinking time.*

(11) *When planning how to achieve a given outcome, I*
   a) *take the resources at my disposal into account (people, equipment, time, and money) and tailor the plan accordingly.*
   b) *devise the plan and then estimate the resources required to achieve it.*
   c) *a bit of both.*

(12) *I make a habit of*
   a) *keeping my desk / work station tidy.*
   b) *having everything I need at hand on my desk.*
   c) *operating with a "clear desk" policy.*

▲▲

▲▲

(13) The nature of my work is such that
   a) it defies quantitative measurement.
   b) it can be quantitatively measured.
   c) some parts of it can be measured, but many key aspects can not.

(14) When tasks are delegated, I believe
   a) the delegatee becomes accountable.
   b) both delegatee and delegator are accountable.
   c) the delegator remains accountable.

(15) I prefer to
   a) "sell" people my ideas.
   b) let a consensus emerge.
   c) get other people's ideas and then make up my mind.

(16) When things go well, I feel pleased and
   a) move on to the next task.
   b) make sure my success has been noted.
   c) review the reasons for the success.

(17) When it is necessary to make a decision that requires an element of discretion (i.e., there isn't a "right" answer), I
   a) feel uncertain which way to go and prefer to sound out other people's opinions.
   b) find my values help me to make a sound decision.
   c) refer it up — ask my boss.

(18) I check whether my short-term goals are compatible with my long-term objectives
   a) often.
   b) sometimes.
   c) rarely.

(19) When I have a plan of action, I
   a) consider its consequences before implementation.
   b) implement it and adjust it "in flight" if circumstances dictate.
   c) both.

(20) Each day I
   a) react flexibly to whatever crops up or whatever I am asked to do.
   b) make a list of priority tasks to be accomplished.
   c) both.

(21) When assessing my contribution, I have
   a) objective/"real" ways to measure the quantity of my work output.
   b) subjective/"gut feel" ways to measure the quantity of my work.
   c) a mixture of both.

(22) I believe that
   a) my boss is responsible for my performance and for my development.
   b) I am responsible for my performance and for my development.
   c) my performance is up to me, but my development is up to my boss.

(23) When people oppose me, I
   a) argue the point.
   b) suggest a compromise.
   c) question them to understand their reasons.

(24) If asked "what did you learn last week?" I would
   a) find it impossible to give a convincing answer.
   b) be able to describe some lessons learned.
   c) be able to describe what I'd done, but be less clear what I'd learned.

▼▼

(continues)

Figure E-2 (Continued.)

25) I usually
   a) strike a balance between the demands of home and work.
   b) make home a priority.
   c) make work a priority.

26) People who know me well would describe me as
   a) a thinker (i.e., someone who ponders and reflects before getting into action).
   b) a doer (i.e., someone who gets into action more quickly).
   c) a mixture of both.

27) When I have produced a plan, I tend to
   a) regard it as a blueprint for action and resist attempts to change it.
   b) regard it as a guide for action and expect to have to change it.
   c) agree to changes with great reluctance.

28) At any point in time
   a) I am crystal clear where my priorities lie.
   b) my priorities are in a state of flux.
   c) a mixture of both.

29) When assessing my contribution, I have
   a) objective ways to measure the quality of my work.
   b) subjective ways of measuring the quality of my work.
   c) a mixture of both.

30) When a mistake has been made, I
   a) engage in damage control activities.
   b) inform my boss and others who will be affected.
   c) wait until a problem emerges.

31) When persuading people to do what I want them to do, I
   a) tell them loud and clear what I want.
   b) let them persuade themselves.
   c) concentrate on the benefits for them.

32) I learn from experience
   a) effortlessly and intuitively.
   b) deliberately and consciously.
   c) a mixture of both.

33) I am the sort of person who tends to be
   a) dissatisfied with the status quo.
   b) accepting of the status quo.
   c) sometimes one, sometimes the other.

34) When setting goals, I tend to
   a) concentrate on setting clear, short-term objectives.
   b) take the longer-term vision into account.
   c) a bit of both.

35) When organizing a decision-making meeting, I
   a) take steps to ensure that the meeting will "rubber-stamp" the decision I want.
   b) plan the venue, time, objectives, agenda, etc., to make it likely that the optimum decision is reached.
   c) send out notification of the time, place, and topic, and leave everything else to be hammered out at the meeting itself.

36) I am
   a) purposeful and eliminate activities that don't fit in with my priorities.
   b) pliable and take on activities that don't necessarily fit in with my objectives.
   c) obliging and just can't say no.

▲▲

(37) *When there are quantity and/or quality problems with work, I assume that they are*
    a) *primarily caused by human fallibility.*
    b) *primarily caused by inadequate systems and procedures.*
    c) *caused by a 50/50 mixture of both.*

(38) *I believe responsibilities are*
    a) *what you take.*
    b) *what you are given.*
    c) *a mixture of both.*

(39) *When setting out to persuade people, I think it is important to*
    a) *assume they have some misgivings and need to be reassured.*
    b) *assume they have major objections and plan how to overcome them.*
    c) *establish their starting position.*

(40) *After I have accomplished something, I prefer to*
    a) *assume I have learned from the experience and move on to the next task.*
    b) *review my experiences carefully in order to pinpoint some "lessons learned".*
    c) *work out how to do even better next time.*

(41) *If questioned about my values, I would*
    a) *be clear about some, but vague about others.*
    b) *be able to articulate them unhesitatingly.*
    c) *find it difficult to communicate them.*

(42) *When I have a decision to make, I*
    a) *follow a logical, systematic process.*
    b) *base it on past precedent.*
    c) *am guided by an intuitive feel for what will/will not work.*

(43) *Before doing something, I*
    a) *ask "who is going to do this, when, and at what cost?"*
    b) *assume it has to be done regardless.*
    c) *often feel resources are inadequate, but to raise this as an issue would be regarded as being negative.*

(44) *When setting priorities, I*
    a) *build in contingency time to allow for unexpected events and interruptions.*
    b) *leave no slack because I'm determined to safeguard my priorities.*
    c) *just have to be flexible whatever priorities I've set.*

(45) *I believe*
    a) *the nature of my work is such that it can be assessed only subjectively.*
    b) *it is possible to measure my work activities.*
    c) *a mixture of both.*

(46) *When something needs to be done, I'm the sort of person who*
    a) *gets clearance before taking the necessary action.*
    b) *does it and informs interested parties later.*
    c) *weighs up the consequences and, if they are high-risk, gets clearance.*

(47) *I am the sort of person who*
    a) *easily establishes rapport with a wide range of different types of people.*
    b) *finds it easy to establish rapport with like-minded people.*
    c) *finds it difficult to establish rapport except with a close circle of people.*

(48) *When a mistake has been made, I tend to*
    a) *conduct a post-mortem to establish how the mistake occurred and who was to blame.*
    b) *work out a robust defence.*
    c) *concentrate on understanding what happened in order to do better/differently in future.*

▽▼

(continues)

Figure E-2   (Continued.)

▲▲

Part Two

Remember to mark
ONE circle ON
THE ANSWER
SHEET PROVID-
ED.

Example:
a) ○

b) ●

c) ○

Please DO NOT
make any marks on
the questionnaire
itself.

49) In my organization, when something happens that isn't covered by procedures, you are expected to
   a) point out the absence of an appropriate procedure.
   b) refer it up for a decision.
   c) use your discretion to decide what to do within certain parameters.

50) I work in an organization where
   a) the long-term strategy is made clear to all.
   b) the long-term strategy is clear only to a few at the top.
   c) there isn't anything that could be called a strategy — other than to carry on doing what we've always done.

51) I work in an organization where
   a) it's a constant battle to secure adequate resources.
   b) adequate resources are provided to secure key objectives.
   c) sometimes a), sometimes b).

52) In my organization,
   a) you set priorities, but demands from seniors alter them.
   b) your priorities are agreed, and seniors help you stick to them.
   c) when seniors make demands, they take your priorities into account.

53) In my organization,
   a) deviations from quality standards become apparent when things go wrong or customers complain, etc.,
   b) deviations from quality standards are constantly monitored.
   c) a mixture of both.

54) In my organization, parameters are set that
   a) restrict your room for maneuver in deciding how best to achieve your objectives.
   b) prescribe your objectives and the means to achieve them.
   c) allow freedom of movement in deciding how best to achieve your objectives.

55) Managers in my organization tend to be
   a) formal and dictatorial: "we are told".
   b) approachable and consultative: "we have input".
   c) participative and collaborative: "we decide together".

56) My organization tends to encourage people to
   a) conform and follow the rules.
   b) experiment and try different ways of doing things.
   c) try things out so long as there is little risk.

57) The organization I work in
   a) has a shared sense of direction and purpose captured in a written mission statement or the like.
   b) assumes we have a shared sense of direction and purpose, but has nothing formalized into a mission statement.
   c) has no agreed longer-term vision.

58) In my organization,
   a) there are planning cycles and procedures that require us to think ahead.
   b) the focus is more on the short-term: this week, this month, this quarter.
   c) we react rather than plan.

59) My organization
   a) plans rigidly.
   b) plans flexibly.
   c) a mixture of both.

60) I work in an organization where
   a) the goal posts keep moving.
   b) you set your own priorities.
   c) priorities are spelled out clearly.

▼▼

▲▼▲

(61) I work in an organization where
    a) quality is a prime responsibility of a quality control function/department/inspector.
    b) people are encouraged to take responsibility for the quality of their work.
    c) quantity takes precedence over quality.

(62) The culture of my organization assumes people work best if they are
    a) directed and controlled.
    b) empowered (i.e., self-directed).
    c) constantly kept under pressure.

(63) Top managers in my organization tend to be
    a) charismatic leaders from the front.
    b) low-profile leaders from behind.
    c) participating and involving.

(64) My organization
    a) pays lip service to the process of continuous improvement.
    b) expects each person to adopt a continuous improvement philosophy.
    c) actively encourages and supports the process of continuous improvement.

(65) The organization I work in has
    a) explicit, shared values and vision set out in writing.
    b) values and vision that are widely understood but not written down.
    c) tacit values and vision that it is assumed people understand.

(66) My organization puts a high priority
    a) on forecasting and planning activities.
    b) on achieving in the "here and now".
    c) on both a) and b) equally.

(67) I work in an organization where deadlines are
    a) set regardless of whether they are achievable with the resources available.
    b) rarely placed on actions.
    c) set, taking due account of resources.

(68) In my organization
    a) important things are planned and not allowed to become urgent.
    b) everything is always urgent/needed "by yesterday".
    c) we don't differentiate between important and urgent.

(69) The culture of my organization
    a) puts quality first.
    b) puts both quality and quantity first.
    c) puts quantity first.

(70) In my organization, responsibilities are delegated
    a) with the authority necessary to do the task.
    b) so that you are not sure how far you can go.
    c) with strings attached.

(71) In my organization, you are expected to
    a) comply.
    b) challenge.
    c) comply or challenge, depending on who it is.

(72) In my organization top managers demonstrate their commitment to training and development by
    a) providing people with ample learning opportunities.
    b) saying how important it is and making the "right noises".
    c) getting actively involved themselves.

▲▼▲

(continues)

Figure E-2 (Continued.)

73) In my organization, the vision
   a) comes down from the top.
   b) is left to you.
   c) is arrived at via a participative process.

74) My organization tends to be
   a) more reactive than proactive.
   b) equally reactive and proactive.
   c) more proactive than reactive.

75) My organization constantly strives to
   a) match resources (time, people, equipment, and money) to the tasks to be done.
   b) find a compromise.
   c) get tasks done despite inadequate resources.

76) I work in an organization where
   a) there are formal systems/procedures to identify and agree on priorities.
   b) priorities emerge in the normal course of events.
   c) priorities are left to individuals.

77) In my organization, we
   a) constantly question whether it is necessary to aim for such high productivity and quality standards.
   b) constantly question which of our current activities are necessary to maintain high productivity and quality.
   c) rarely question such things.

78) In my organization,
   a) we have rules, regulations, and conventions to cover all eventualities.
   b) there are plenty of rules, regulations, and conventions.
   c) there are few fixed rules, regulations, or conventions.

79) In my organization, important decisions
   a) are usually taken in secret and announced as a "fait accompli".
   b) the issues are usually debated openly before decisions are taken.
   c) are arrived at by consensus.

80) My organization
   a) provides people with planned learning/developmental opportunities.
   b) provides opportunities on a "sink or swim" basis.
   c) a mixture of both.

81) If questioned about my organization's values, I would
   a) find it difficult to give a coherent answer.
   b) have to refer to the mission statement as a reminder.
   c) be able to describe them.

82) I work in an organization where once goals are set,
   a) the focus remains on them, with few distractions from the chosen direction.
   b) many factors are likely to cause them to be modified.
   c) we often lose sight of the reasons why activities are being carried out.

83) In my organization
   a) there are intermittent campaigns to check on the cost-effectiveness of resource utilization.
   b) there is a continuous quest to find ways to use time and resources more cost-effectively.
   c) cost-effectiveness is rarely questioned.

84) The culture of my organization
   a) actively encourages systematic time management, the use of personal organizers, and the like.
   b) leaves individuals free to decide how best to organize themselves and manage their time.
   c) is not time and self-management conscious.

85) In my organization, priority is primarily put on
   a) solving problems caused by deviations from quality standards.
   b) preventing deviations from quality standards.
   c) both equally.

86) In my organization,
   a) you are encouraged to find new ways to do your work.
   b) you are expected to follow laid-down guidelines when doing your work.
   c) a mixture of both.

87) I would describe my organization as a place where
   a) it is wise to filter anything resembling bad news.
   b) you need to weigh up when to be open and honest and when to be more "diplomatic".
   c) trust is high, and you can be open and honest — even with bad news.

88) I work in an organization where
   a) you are actively encouraged to share what you have learned widely.
   b) your boss reviews what you have learned periodically.
   c) no one shows much interest in what you have learned.

89) My organization
   a) expects you to balance the demands of home and work.
   b) understands that home demands can take priority.
   c) expects you to eat, sleep, and breathe your work.

90) My organization
   a) offers tools/techniques/procedures to help you think strategically.
   b) puts the emphasis on strategic thinking.
   c) leaves you to your own devices when thinking strategically.

91) In my organization,
   a) resources are never adequate no matter how convincing a case you make for more.
   b) if you make a convincing case, adequate resources are allocated.
   c) you are expected to do the best you can with what you've got.

92) In my organization,
   a) plans, once drawn up, tend to be sacrosanct.
   b) plans are constantly updated and revised in the light of events.
   c) plans seldom relate to what we actually do.

93) In my organization, greater emphasis is placed on
   a) installing systems and procedures to ensure the repeatability of high quality work.
   b) urging people to be quality conscious and try harder.
   c) a mixture of both.

94) In my organization
   a) job descriptions go into meticulous detail.
   b) job descriptions are very general and leave plenty of scope for flexibility.
   c) there are no job descriptions as such.

95) In my organization, interpersonal skills are considered to be
   a) desirable but not essential.
   b) matters of style, not substance.
   c) as important as technical expertise.

96) In my organization,
   a) it is assumed that you will learn from experience relatively unaided.
   b) providing feedback, coaching, and appraising are a way of life.
   c) feedback, coaching, and appraising happen annually as part of the formal appraisal process.

PLEASE ENSURE THAT ALL ITEMS HAVE BEEN ANSWERED BEFORE RETURNING THE ANSWER SHEET AND QUESTIONNAIRE. REMEMBER TO WRITE YOUR NAME ON THE ANSWER SHEET.

(continues)

Figure E-2 (Continued.)

THE EFFECTIVENESS QUESTIONNAIRE
PROCESS-SKILLS ANALYSIS™

ANSWER SHEET

There are three possible answers to each question: a, b, or c. When you have decided which answer is most true for you, mark the appropriate circle on this answer sheet. Choose only ONE item per question.

Example: 1. a) ○
           b) ●
           c) ○

1.	13.	25.	37.	49.	61.	73.	85.
a) ○ b) ○ c) ○	a) ○ b) ○ c) ○	a) ○ b) ○ c) ○	a) ○ b) ○ c) ○	a) ○ b) ○ c) ○	a) ○ b) ○ c) ○	a) ○ b) ○ c) ○	a) ○ b) ○ c) ○
2.	14.	26.	38.	50.	62.	74.	86.
a) ○ b) ○ c) ○	a) ○ b) ○ c) ○	a) ○ b) ○ c) ○	a) ○ b) ○ c) ○	a) ○ b) ○ c) ○	a) ○ b) ○ c) ○	a) ○ b) ○ c) ○	a) ○ b) ○ c) ○
3.	15.	27.	39.	51.	63.	75.	87.
a) ○ b) ○ c) ○	a) ○ b) ○ c) ○	a) ○ b) ○ c) ○	a) ○ b) ○ c) ○	a) ○ b) ○ c) ○	a) ○ b) ○ c) ○	a) ○ b) ○ c) ○	a) ○ b) ○ c) ○
4.	16.	28.	40.	52.	64.	76.	88.
a) ○ b) ○ c) ○	a) ○ b) ○ c) ○	a) ○ b) ○ c) ○	a) ○ b) ○ c) ○	a) ○ b) ○ c) ○	a) ○ b) ○ c) ○	a) ○ b) ○ c) ○	a) ○ b) ○ c) ○
5.	17.	29.	41.	53.	65.	77.	89.
a) ○ b) ○ c) ○	a) ○ b) ○ c) ○	a) ○ b) ○ c) ○	a) ○ b) ○ c) ○	a) ○ b) ○ c) ○	a) ○ b) ○ c) ○	a) ○ b) ○ c) ○	a) ○ b) ○ c) ○
6.	18.	30.	42.	54.	66.	78.	90.
a) ○ b) ○ c) ○	a) ○ b) ○ c) ○	a) ○ b) ○ c) ○	a) ○ b) ○ c) ○	a) ○ b) ○ c) ○	a) ○ b) ○ c) ○	a) ○ b) ○ c) ○	a) ○ b) ○ c) ○
7.	19.	31.	43.	55.	67.	79.	91.
a) ○ b) ○ c) ○	a) ○ b) ○ c) ○	a) ○ b) ○ c) ○	a) ○ b) ○ c) ○	a) ○ b) ○ c) ○	a) ○ b) ○ c) ○	a) ○ b) ○ c) ○	a) ○ b) ○ c) ○
8.	20.	32.	44.	56.	68.	80.	92.
a) ○ b) ○ c) ○	a) ○ b) ○ c) ○	a) ○ b) ○ c) ○	a) ○ b) ○ c) ○	a) ○ b) ○ c) ○	a) ○ b) ○ c) ○	a) ○ b) ○ c) ○	a) ○ b) ○ c) ○
9.	21.	33.	45.	57.	69.	81.	93.
a) ○ b) ○ c) ○	a) ○ b) ○ c) ○	a) ○ b) ○ c) ○	a) ○ b) ○ c) ○	a) ○ b) ○ c) ○	a) ○ b) ○ c) ○	a) ○ b) ○ c) ○	a) ○ b) ○ c) ○
10.	22.	34.	46.	58.	70.	82.	94.
a) ○ b) ○ c) ○	a) ○ b) ○ c) ○	a) ○ b) ○ c) ○	a) ○ b) ○ c) ○	a) ○ b) ○ c) ○	a) ○ b) ○ c) ○	a) ○ b) ○ c) ○	a) ○ b) ○ c) ○
11.	23.	35.	47.	59.	71.	83.	95.
a) ○ b) ○ c) ○	a) ○ b) ○ c) ○	a) ○ b) ○ c) ○	a) ○ b) ○ c) ○	a) ○ b) ○ c) ○	a) ○ b) ○ c) ○	a) ○ b) ○ c) ○	a) ○ b) ○ c) ○
12.	24.	36.	48.	60.	72.	84.	96.
a) ○ b) ○ c) ○	a) ○ b) ○ c) ○	a) ○ b) ○ c) ○	a) ○ b) ○ c) ○	a) ○ b) ○ c) ○	a) ○ b) ○ c) ○	a) ○ b) ○ c) ○	a) ○ b) ○ c) ○

High-Performance Superstars

What does our study of knowledge worker competencies tell us? As a by-product of four years of research into the productivity of knowledge workers, we have found that high-performance workers share these common characteristics:

• When they make decisions, they make them with the *end in mind*. This comes from a clear vision of what the corporation is trying to achieve. Here management must play a critical role in creating a mission statement that crystallizes the company's key business goals. This should not be framed and hung on the wall like a piece of office art, but instead must be communicated over and over again through memos, newsletters, and meetings. This helps everyone to make decisions with the end in mind.

• They create *action plans* designed to implement the company's mission. Typically, star performers establish precisely what they intend to accomplish in specific time frames, such as one month, six months, a year. Although they remain focused on these time-sensitive objectives, they remain flexible enough to change their tactics if business conditions or the prevailing economic environment change. For example, assume that a general manager is seeking to increase profits by 5 percent over the course of a year, mostly by increasing sales. Then bang, a recession hits in midstream. Rather than throwing in the towel, she sticks to her profit goal, but focuses more intensely on cutting expenses than on increasing sales. To do this, she reviews the company's procedures with an eye toward engineering the assembly line to wring excess costs out of the system. In this way, the manager stays focused on her objective, but pursues new means of achieving it.

• Turning *intentions into actions*, they muster the resources necessary to accomplish their action plans. First, they determine what they will need—raw materials, additional employees, creative input, capital, alliances inside and outside of the company. Then they act to assemble these resources in a way that makes the work process more efficient.

For example, a sales manager who is determined to speed

shipments to customers may create an alliance with the warehouse supervisor, promising faster sales and reorder data in return for accelerated order processing. The bottom line: There is greater collaboration among the company's employees, resulting in realization of its goals and greater creativity.

• They are good at ordering priorities to reflect the company's objectives. Their thinking goes like this: "Here's what I am going to do today. This task is a top priority not because it is the project I want most to clear from my desk, or because someone is pressing me to do it, but because it will draw the straightest line between my work and the company's goals."

• They are skilled at balancing the quality/quantity equation that is inherent in all work. For example, a well-intentioned but relatively unproductive employee may take pride in saying, "I always do everything perfectly." When management counters that the quest for perfection caused the company to miss the deadline for a key delivery, he returns to the same myopic theme: "Yes, but you have to admit my work was done beautifully."

Recognizing instinctively that this is unacceptable, the best performers strive to achieve the delicate balance between quality and quantity. This means doing the best work in the time frame and the quantities required to meet the customer's expectations and the company's strategic goals.

• They take ownership of the projects and responsibilities assigned to them. Consider this the corporate version of Harry Truman's legendary statement, "The buck stops here." Superior performers have a "can do" attitude. They rarely shun responsibility. Instead, they consider completion of a project to be a personal responsibility, and they work to influence others along the assembly line to help achieve stated goals (which, as we have noted, are always linked to the company's objectives).

Assume, for example, that your MIS manager is asked to produce monthly reports tracking the company's sales trends. Soon after the manager sets out to generate the data, he faces a roadblock: An administrator in the sales department is reluctant to release the necessary reports on a timely basis. Rather than pointing a finger at the administrator and taking a "don't blame me" attitude, the MIS manager goes through back channels to tap new sources of data, making certain that the reports are produced on time. Because he "owned" the project, he refused to let it be derailed. This resourcefulness and determination makes the super performer an unstoppable and powerful force for increased productivity.

By identifying the traits and characteristics of the super performers in your business and by seeking to train everyone in the skills they exhibit, you will be reengineering your work processes (your *invisible assembly line*) for maximum productivity and profits.

To receive sample forms described in this book, please call 1-800-221-9031 and ask for the IAL Department.

Appendix

The Development and Validity of the P-SA

As we have noted, the Process-Skills Analysis is the key to measuring the process-skill efficiency of individuals, teams, and organizations engaged in knowledge work. It is based on a theoretical model of knowledge work.

The model was originally established based both on a thorough review of management research and literature, as well as on a rigorous empirical study into the skills, competencies, and behaviors that distinguish the highest performing knowledge workers from their mediocre- and low-performing counterparts. The two-year study, which was conducted in one of the largest fifteen industrial corporations in the world, involved extensive observation of knowledge workers and teams as they performed their daily tasks, and a comprehensive interview process. This study, combined with the aforementioned review of management research, uncovered the basic multi-tiered structure of knowledge work, comprising ten fundamental process skills, twenty-five core competencies, and 308 observable knowledge worker behaviors.

Once developed, the initial conceptual model was the object of intense scrutiny. Expert judgment and informal pilot tests led to a reduction in the number of process skills to eight, core competencies to twenty-three and behavioral items to 258. Each of the behavioral items was then assigned to one of the eight process-skill categories.

Based on the above research, the initial version of the P-SA was developed in February 1993. The subsequent process of instrument enhancement involved the collection of data from a diverse sample population of knowledge workers and extensive analyses employing sophisticated statistical techniques.

The first cycle of data analysis was based on the P-SA results of 1,200 knowledge workers. These workers, representing a wide range of countries, industries, occupations, age groups, income brackets, and cultures, as well as both sexes, were deliberately selected to produce a generalizable sample of data.

The reservoir of sample data was then subjected to a barrage of formal statistical tests. These included internal consistency, interscale correlation, response strength, and cluster analytic studies. In addition, discrimination tests were performed to identify all items that did not properly distinguish between high, low, and moderately performing workers. Any items that elicited a disproportionate share of like responses (above 60 percent) failed this selection process.

The results of the above tests prompted the instrument developers to modify certain items, transfer others to different process-skill categories, and eliminate others from the questionnaire altogether. In total, twelve behavioral items were completely removed, lowering the final number to 246.

These modifications generated a theoretically sound, highly reliable, and thoroughly validated psychometric instrument. Over the 1993–1995 period, the revised version of the P-SA was completed by a heterogeneous sample of over 7,500 knowledge workers. At the end of this period, the earlier statistical tests were repeated, and additional analyses were performed to verify the P-SA's psychometric properties. The results of these tests are presented in this report.

The P-SA, then, underwent a rigorous development process, ensuring its overall efficacy and dependability as a skill measurement instrument.

The P-SA Effectiveness Questionnaire

The P-SA Effectiveness Questionnaire comprises ninety-six behaviorally based multiple choice questions. The questionnaire consists of two parts, the first of which focuses on the respondent's own behaviors and practices. A sample item from Part One is as follows:

> When setting out to persuade people, I think it is important to:
>
> a) Assume they have some misgivings and need to be reassured.
> b) Assume they have major objections and plan to overcome them.
> c) Establish their starting position.

The second part of the questionnaire focuses on the respondent's perception of the behaviors and practices of the organization or team in which he or she works. A sample item from Part Two is as follows:

> I work in an organization where:
>
> a) The long-term strategy is made clear to all.
> b) The long-term strategy is clear only to a few at the top.
> c) There isn't anything that could be called a strategy, other than to carry on doing what we've always done.

The questionnaire generally takes in the range of thirty to forty minutes to complete.

P-SA Scoring System

Each P-SA Effectiveness Questionnaire multiple choice item offers three behavioral alternatives, one of which is indicative of superlative performance, one of moderate performance, and one of low performance. Each alternative, in turn, corresponds to a given number of points: ten for the ideal behavior, five for the moderately effective practice, and one for the least-effective habit.

Six behavioral questions correspond to each process skill. Therefore, the maximum number of points available per skill area is sixty, the minimum number six. Increasing scores within that range indicates higher levels of process-skill proficiency.

Each respondent, then, receives an individual raw score out of sixty for each process skill and a similar raw score out of sixty for each organizational process skill.

Three main performance quotients (the Effectiveness Quotient, the Learning Quotient, and the Knowledge Quotient) are derived from these raw process-skill scores. The Effectiveness Quotient, rated on a scale of 0–100, is an indicator of current performance based on the average of the scores achieved in the eight process-skill areas. The next key index, the Learning Quotient, is a measure of willingness and ability to learn from experience. It is rated on a scale of 0–1.0 and is based on a combination of the Continuous Improvement raw score and several additional learning-related item scores. The final indicator is the Knowledge Quotient, an index of current and potential for future effectiveness. Rated on a scale of 0–1000, it is derived from the average of the raw scores on the preceding two quotients.

Individual and organizational process-skill and performance-quotient averages have been established based on a sample population of 8,342 P-SA responses. The average individual raw process-skill scores (see Figure A-1) vary in magnitude from 35 for Defining Performance Expectations (Q^2 Factoring) to 45 for Continuous Improvement. Figure A-1 compares the average individual scores (out of 60) in each of the eight fundamental process skills. A score of 40 is consistent with moderate effectiveness in each area. The average organizational raw scores (see Figure A-2) follow a similar trend. Figure A-2 compares the average organization scores (out of 60) in each of the eight fundamental process skills. They vary from 35 for Managing Priorities to 43 for Taking Ownership. The international averages used in Figures A-1 and A-2 are based on different volume population samples than those used in the P-SA Effectiveness Profile.

The average individual performance quotient scores for Ef-

Figure A-1. Process-skills average scores: individual.

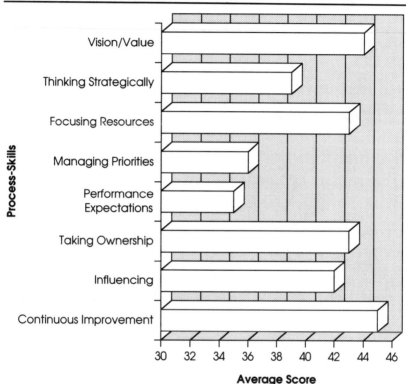

fectiveness, Learning, and Knowledge are 68.3, 0.73, and 506 respectively (see Figure A-3). The table outlines average individual and organization scores in each of the three performance quotients. These results suggest that knowledge workers tend, on average, to be no better than moderately effective in the eight fundamental process skills. The average organization performance quotient scores (again, see Figure A-3) are 63.9 for Effectiveness, 0.65 for Learning, and 443 for Knowledge. These results indicate that organizations and teams are typically perceived by knowledge workers as being only somewhat effective.

These data tend to confirm the hypothesis that knowledge workers, teams, and organizations are, on the whole, poorly equipped to deal with the rigors and challenges of the New Economy.

Figure A-2. Process-skills average scores: organization.

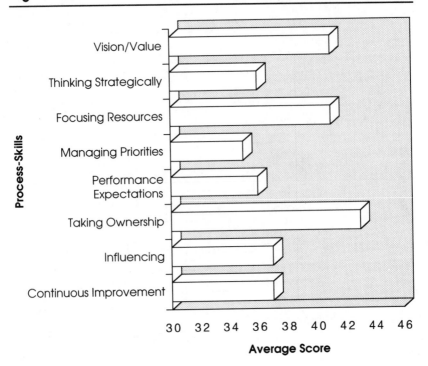

Figure A-3. Knowledge quotient average scores.

	Individual	Organization
Effectiveness Quotient	68.30	63.90
Learning Quotient	0.73	0.65
Knowledge Quotient	506.00	443.00

P-SA International Database

As mentioned, the majority of the statistical tests and studies contained in this report are based on an exceptionally diverse population sample of 8,342 knowledge workers (see Figures A-4, A-5, A-6, and A-7). Of this sample population, 64 percent are male and 36 percent are female. The majority make between $20,000 and $80,000 per year, are between thirty and fifty years of age, and have over ten years of experience in the workforce.

Figure A-4. Demographic breakdown: income.

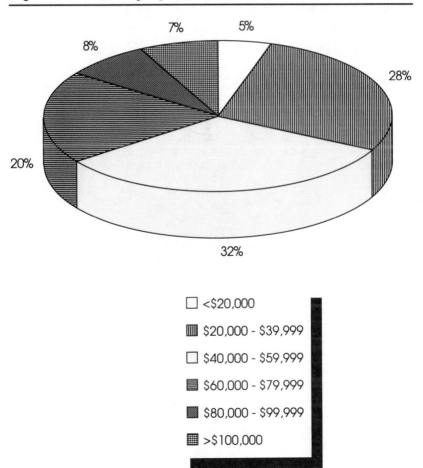

□ <$20,000

▥ $20,000 - $39,999

□ $40,000 - $59,999

▤ $60,000 - $79,999

▨ $80,000 - $99,999

▦ >$100,000

Figure A-5. Demographic breakdown by sex.

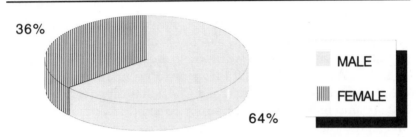

36%

64%

MALE

FEMALE

Figure A-6. Demographic breakdown by age.

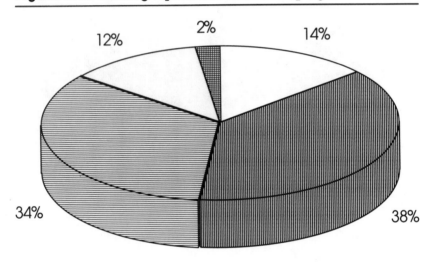

12%   2%   14%

34%   38%

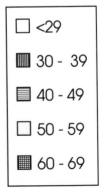

☐ <29

▦ 30 - 39

▤ 40 - 49

☐ 50 - 59

▦ 60 - 69

Figure A-7. Demographic breakdown by work experience.

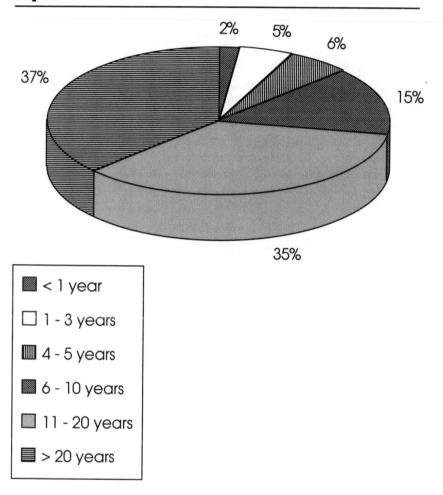

A vast array of industry groups, including manufacturing, natural resources, education, wholesale/retail, banking/finance, construction, government, insurance, professional, transportation, high technology, real estate, health care, and business services are represented in the sample. The manufacturing and government industries are the most widely represented, comprising 17 percent and 11 percent of the population base respectively. The sample population contains knowledge workers from fifteen countries (the United States, Canada, Australia, New Zealand, Scotland, Ireland, Brazil, England, Hong Kong, Singapore, Holland, France, Belgium, Mexico, and Columbia) on five continents.

Figures A-4 through A-7 outline the various percentage demographic breakdowns according to income (Figure A-4), sex (Figure A-5), age (Figure A-6), and work experience (Figure A-7).

While no attempts have been made to generate representative sample populations of knowledge workers, the large size of the sample group described in this Appendix ensures the widespread applicability of any resulting findings.

Reliability of the P-SA

To be useful and accurate, psychological, educational, personality, and skill assessment instruments must be consistent or reliable in what they measure. The concept of *reliability* refers to the degree to which scores are free from unsystematic or random errors of measurement—that is, errors that differ from person to person during any one testing session or that vary from time to time for a given person measured twice by the same instrument. A test-taker usually will perform differently on one occasion than on another, or on two forms of a test that are intended to be interchangeable, for reasons such as anxiety, fatigue, and test-taking conditions—all unrelated to the actual purpose of the test. These differences are to a certain extent unavoidable. However, other random differences between scores from one occasion to another—specifically those that result from structural flaws or inconsistencies in the given instrument—are not only avoidable, but completely unacceptable. These score inconsistencies reduce the reliability of the score obtained for a person from a single measurement.

There are two fundamental aspects to reliability: internal consistency and stability over time.

Internal Consistency

If all the items (behavioral questions) that make up a given scale (process skill) are homogenous (i.e., measure the same thing, as inclusion in a single scale would suggest) then that scale is said to be internally consistent. Individuals who achieve high scores on one of the behaviors that makes up an internally consistent scale should also score well in the remaining behavioral areas that define that scale. This is an indication that item responses are concordant, and, therefore, that the scale itself is relatively free from unwanted random measurement errors.

Measures of internal consistency (of which there are many) are based on the average correlation among items within a scale. *Cronbach's alpha coefficient* is both the most commonly used and widely accepted measure of internal consistency. In theory, alpha coefficients may range in value from -1 to 1, with sub-zero values indicating inconsistencies among items within a scale and positive values indicating consistencies. An alpha coefficient of .7 is generally considered optimal for a development instrument such as the P-SA.

Internal consistency analyses were performed on the sample population data of the 8,342 P-SA respondents using Cronbach's alpha coefficient. The internal consistency tests were applied to three sets of P-SA data: organization scores, self-perception individual scores, and colleague perception individual scores. The results of the tests are charted in Figure A-8. The figure outlines internal consistency scores for the individual and organization components of the P-SA. The results indicate that the items comprising each process skill tend to measure the same domain of interest.

The internal consistency scores range in value from .497 (Influencing) to .748 (Continuous Improvement) for the organizational component of the P-SA. For the individual component, colleague perception internal consistency scores, which range from .11 (Focusing Resources) to .71 (Influencing) are, as expected, slightly higher than the self-perception scores, which extend from .05 (Taking Ownership) to .50 (Managing Priorities). Values of this magnitude confirm that the items compris-

Figure A-8. Internal consistency.

	Individual		Organization
	Colleague	*Self*	
Values/Vision	0.14	0.18	0.58
Thinking Strategically	0.28	0.3	0.73
Focusing Resources	0.11	0.28	0.55
Managing Priorities	0.41	0.5	0.63
Performance Expectations	0.56	0.49	0.56
Taking Ownership	0.46	0.05	0.5
Influencing	0.71	0.34	0.68
Continuous Improvement	0.14	0.33	0.75

ing each process skill do, in fact, tend to measure the same domain of interest.

Certain factors or "contingent variables" might lead the above coefficients to underestimate the instrument's actual internal consistency. Among the most significant of these factors is the incidence of guessing. On a multiple-choice instrument such as the P-SA, an individual, who does not really know the answers to two closely related questions, may guess incorrectly on one and correctly on the other. Purely by chance, then, the individual's responses to like questions will vary, the overall effect of which is to artificially lower the instrument's internal consistency coefficients. Cronbach's alpha coefficients, then, significantly underestimate the internal consistency of the P-SA.

Most competitor diagnostic instruments employ Likert-type measurement scales to assess respondent skill levels, and, therefore, are not subject to the same inaccuracies in the measurement of internal consistency that will so often arise in the application of Cronbach's formula to multiple choice questionnaires. Those that employ a Likert measurement scale generate alpha values that may appear artificially inflated relative to those of the P-SA.

Stability Over Time

The stability of psychometric instrument scores over relatively short periods of time is an important aspect of reliability. The scales of which an instrument is composed should be sufficiently stable to produce similar responses on two different occasions, assuming that no significant event, such as training, takes place in the interim. If the items within a scale are unclear or easily misinterpreted, however, they may generate varying responses over time. The resulting instability in scale scores signifies a low overall instrument reliability.

The most common measure of instrument stability is the test/retest coefficient of correlation, which involves measuring the score correlation between consecutive administrations of a given instrument to the same individual. Theoretically, test/retest reliability coefficients can range fom -1.0 to 1.0. In practice, however, they generally fall between .3 and .8, with .7 generally being considered acceptably high.

The P-SA test/retest study generated overwhelmingly positive results (see Figure A-9). A sample of thirty knowledge workers from two countries and of varying ages completed the P-SA Effectiveness Questionnaire, and, within two weeks, were retested. Respondents were not allowed to review their initial

Figure A-9. Test/retest reliability.

	Individual	Organization
Values/Vision	0.9	0.59
Thinking Strategically	0.92	0.69
Focusing Resources	0.84	0.8
Managing Priorities	0.91	0.83
Performance Expectations	0.88	0.81
Taking Ownership	0.92	0.77
Influencing	0.84	0.72
Continuous Improvement	0.95	0.9

test results or undergo training in the interim time period. On the individual component of the P-SA, test/retest reliability co-efficients ranged from .84 for Focusing Resources and Influencing to .95 for Continuous Improvement. On the organizational component, the reliability coefficients were slightly lower, extending from .59 for Values/Vision to .89 for Continuous Improvement. This data strongly suggest that, barring any systematic individual or organizational training or consulting interventions, P-SA results are inherently stable over time.

The test/retest study may tend to either overestimate or underestimate the true reliability of the P-SA. Test respondents may, then, have completed the initial test, and, in the period prior to the administration of the retest, undergone either skill development or a regression to lower skill levels. Thus, the score discrepancies may represent not measurement error, but fluctuations in skill level, and, to this extent, reliability is underestimated. The test/retest procedure, therefore, may have either underestimated or overestimated the P-SA's reliability, depending on which of the two effects was more significant.

It is important to remember, though, that high reliability is not necessarily synonymous with high validity. One could, for example, seek to measure the intelligence of a sample of children by having them run as fast as possible. Their maximum speeds on one occasion might correlate highly with their maximum speeds on another, and thus, being repeatable, the measure would be highly reliable. But obviously the speed at which children run has no relation to mental agility and so would not constitute a valid measure of intelligence. The amount of unsystematic measurement error places a ceiling on an instrument's validity, but even in the complete absence of such error, there is no guarantee of validity. Therefore, reliability is a necessary but not sufficient condition for validity.

Validity of P-SA Inferences

The most important criterion in the evaluation of psychometric instruments is *validity*. The concept of validity refers to the degree to which the inferences made implicitly or explicitly from an instrument's scores are pertinent, useful, meaningful, relevant, and legitimate. The validation of a psychometric instrument, then, involves amassing empirical and theoretical evidence to support such inferences.

It is important to note that instrument validity is a matter of degree rather than an all-or-none property. No instrument is completely and undeniably valid or, for that matter, completely and undeniably invalid. Additional data must constantly be amassed to further verify the assumptions underlying a given psychometric instrument. The validation process is, then, unending.

The validation of the P-SA involves accumulating support for the three primary inferences that underlie its use. These inferences are that:

1. The P-SA measures process skills.
2. Process skills are intimately related to overall effectiveness.
3. Process skills are amenable to change.

Support for each inference will be provided in turn.

The P-SA Measures Process Skills

The most obvious assumption inherent in the use of the P-SA is that the instrument actually measures process skills. While it is difficult to directly prove that a psychometric tool measures what it purports to measure, several indirect approaches are common. First, it is fundamentally important to establish the instrument's theoretical grounding. The items that make up each scale should, for example, relate to each other conceptually. Moreover, the scales themselves should be embedded in a coherent, logical, and understandable framework.

The P-SA is based on a theoretically sound model of knowledge work. Its scales represent the eight component parts or processes of work—the so-called knowledge-work invisible assembly line. Together, these processes ensure that knowledge work is performed effectively.

The behaviors that make up the P-SA Effectiveness Questionnaire form eight natural clusters, each of which represents a particular work process. A given behavior, then, is closely related to the others in its particular cluster and indicative of some degree of skill in a process area.

A second indirect method of confirming that the P-SA measures process skills is of a statistical nature. Since the P-SA assumes that several conceptually distinct skills make up the overall construct of effectiveness, it is important to prove that each skill area is, in fact, statistically "different." A common technique used to perform this proof is to measure the correlation among the eight process skills. The results of this test are shown in Figure A-10. The tables in the figure detail the statistical correlation between the individual and organization process skills that make up the P-SA. The values range from .62 to .80, confirming that, while each skill is distinct, they have in common their link to overall knowledge worker effectiveness.

The interscale correlation among process skills on the first half of the P-SA range in value from .619 to .691 (ignoring the correlation between like scales), with a weaker statistical relationship existing between Values and Vision and Performance Expectations, and the strongest between Thinking Strategically and Focusing Resources. The correlation among process skills on the second half of the P-SA are moderately higher, ranging from .694 between Performance Expectations and Influencing to .804 between Influencing and Continuous Improvement. The inter–process-skill correlation is consistently strong, confirming that, while each skill is distinct and measures a separate construct, they have in common their link to overall knowledge worker effectiveness.

This theoretical and statistical evidence provides overwhelming support for the notion that the P-SA does, in fact, measure process skills.

Relation of Process Skills to Effectiveness

The most fundamental premise underlying the use of the P-SA is that process skills are linked to overall individual, team, and organizational effectiveness. The standard strategy employed to test this inference is to compare scores on the instrument in

Figure A-10. Inter process-skill correlation.

Individual

	V/V	TS	FR	MP	PE	TO	I	CI
Values/Vision	1.00	0.69	0.69	0.67	0.62	0.67	0.66	0.68
Thinking Strategically	0.69	1.00	0.69	0.68	0.64	0.66	0.66	0.69
Focusing Resources	0.69	0.69	1.00	0.68	0.64	0.67	0.68	0.68
Managing Priorities	0.67	0.68	0.68	1.00	0.64	0.65	0.66	0.67
Performance Expectations	0.62	0.64	0.64	0.64	1.00	0.63	0.62	0.63
Taking Ownership	0.67	0.66	0.67	0.65	0.63	1.00	0.66	0.66
Influencing	0.66	0.66	0.67	0.66	0.62	0.66	1.00	0.67
Continuous Improvement	0.68	0.69	0.68	0.67	0.63	0.66	0.67	1.00

Organization

	V/V	TS	FR	MP	PE	TO	I	CI
Values/Vision	1.00	0.71	0.73	0.74	0.71	0.72	0.74	0.78
Thinking Strategically	0.77	1.00	0.76	0.79	0.73	0.71	0.75	0.79
Focusing Resources	0.73	0.76	1.00	0.76	0.72	0.73	0.75	0.77
Managing Priorities	0.74	0.79	0.76	1.00	0.73	0.71	0.75	0.79
Performance Expectations	0.71	0.73	0.72	0.73	1.00	0.69	0.72	0.75
Taking Ownership	0.72	0.71	0.73	0.71	0.69	1.00	0.76	0.76
Influencing	0.74	0.75	0.75	0.75	0.72	0.76	1.00	0.80
Continuous Improvement	0.78	0.79	0.77	0.79	0.75	0.76	0.80	1.00

question to some other objective variable or measure directly related to effectiveness or bottom-line performance. An immediately available, universally applicable, and widely accepted measure as such, is income.

Prior to the analysis of the sample P-SA data, the authors of this report hypothesized that individual process-skill scores and performance quotients would correlate closely with knowledge worker incomes. Individuals with high process-skill competence, our logic followed, should, by virtue of their competitive advantage, charge to the top of their respective organizations and attract correspondingly high levels of compensation.

In order to test our hypothesis, we subdivided the 8,342 P-SA responses into six major income categories: $0–19,999, $20,000–$39,999, $40,000–$59,999, $60,000–$79,999, $80,000–$99,999, and $100,000 and up. We then derived the average process-skill and quotient scores for each income level and compared the two sets of data. The results are shown in Figure A-11. The chart in the figure outlines the average process-skill and performance scores for each of six income categories. The scores tend to rise with increasing compensation levels.

Not surprisingly, our hypothesis was correct. Increasing income levels are accompanied, on average, by corresponding gains in process-skill and performance quotient scores. While the income-level score variations may not appear large, even the most incremental differences are of tremendous significance when dealing with a sample size as large as ours.

Of particular interest is the rise in Knowledge Quotient scores, the indicators of overall effectiveness (see Figure A-12). The graph displays the rise in Knowledge Quotient scores with increasing compensation levels. A strong link clearly exists between income and P-SA scores. The average Knowledge Quotient starts off at 485 for workers earning less than $20,000 and then rises dramatically with each income level thereafter. The progression culminates in an average quotient score of 536 for workers earning over $100,000. Incidentally, the value of 536 is not only the highest quotient score among the multiple income levels but also the highest value of any demographic group (age, industry, sex, work experience).

In order to lend further credibility to the above test results (to strengthen the link between compensation level and process-skill proficiency) we conducted a similar analysis on a sample of colleague perception P-SA response. We hypothesized that the most effective knowledge workers (that is, those commanding the loftiest incomes) would, all other things being equal, receive the highest average P-SA scores from their colleagues (peers, supervisors, and direct reports).

The test results confirmed our hypothesis. A statistically significant positive correlation exists between colleague proc-

Figure A-11. Income and process skills.

	<$20K	$20K-$39.9K	$40K-$59.9K	$60K-$79.9K	$80K-$99.9K	>$100K
Values/Vision	43.1	43.3	43.9	44.3	44.5	45
Thinking Strategically	37.1	38.1	39	39.5	40.5	41.3
Focusing Resources	40.9	41.5	42.2	43.3	44.6	45.1
Managing Priorities	35.2	34.8	35.5	36.4	37.5	38.2
Performance Expectations	35.4	34.7	35.1	35.2	35.6	36.7
Taking Ownership	41.5	42	43	43.9	44.7	45.2
Influencing	41.8	41.4	42.7	42.9	43	44
Continuous Improvement	44.9	44.7	45.4	45.4	45.7	45.6
Effectiveness Quotient	66.7	66.8	68.1	69	70.1	70.7
Learning Quotient	0.72	0.72	0.73	0.74	0.75	0.75
Knowledge Quotient	485	486	506	514	529	536

Figure A-12. Income and knowledge quotient.

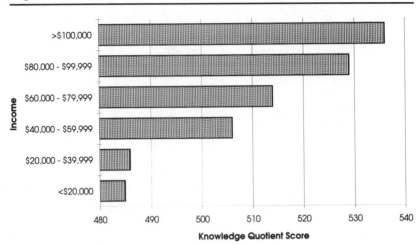

ess-skill ratings and knowledge worker compensation levels. This is highlighted by the fact that, once again, the most handsomely compensated workers (over $100,000 per year) received the highest average Knowledge Quotient score. Clearly, the link between P-SA scores and compensation levels is a strong one.

The results, then, are conclusive. The highest earning knowledge workers, the heads of companies, the leaders of government, the most successful entrepreneurs—those at the forefront of the knowledge revolution—are also the most process-skill proficient.

We can confidently conclude, therefore, that the eight fundamental process skills measured by the P-SA are directly and closely linked to overall individual effectiveness.

Do the same conclusions apply to teams and entire organizations? That is, does a similar correlation exist between process-skill proficiency and team or organizational effectiveness? In order to answer this question, we once again formulated a hypothesis. We postulated that process-skill teams should, over time, achieve superior bottom-line results, a postulate we then tested with three regional teams (western, eastern, and central) from a North American Fortune 50 company. Of the three autonomous teams, all of which were similar in size and functional composition, the western one consistently outshone the others, both in terms of sales and profits over a five-year period. Our hypothesis was that process skills were, at least in part, responsible for the team's high performance. While a myriad of other factors, such as economic conditions, intensity of competition, market size, and access to resources certainly played a role in the high-performing team's relative success, our research led us to believe that these only accounted for a portion of the team's superior performance. For example, while the western team benefited from a healthier economy during the early stages of the measurement period, the eastern and central teams profited from more vibrant economic conditions in the latter stages.

In order to test our hypothesis, we measured and compared the average process-skill levels of the three regional teams. The P-SA results are presented in Figure A-13. The graph highlights the discrepancies in average process-skill scores among three regional teams from the Fortune 50 company. As predicted, the higher performing western team tends to be more process-skill proficient.

As expected, the high-performance team is significantly more process-skill proficient. Of particular significance once again is the discrepancy in Knowledge Quotient scores. The western team's Knowledge Quotient, the ultimate index of knowledge-work team effectiveness, is, in absolute terms, 84 and 132 points higher than the eastern and central team scores, respectively (see Figure A-14). The graph displays the difference in Knowledge Quotient (an overall effectiveness indicator) scores between the three regional teams from the Fortune 50 company. As hypothesized, the western team, which consistently outperformed its counterparts over a five-year period, possesses a significantly higher Knowledge Quotient.

One might argue that the above results establish some relationship between process-skills and bottom-line performance, but that the direction of the relationship is unclear. Perhaps, for example, the western team gained access to additional skill-training dollars by virtue of its financial success. The team's high performance, then, would have resulted in,

Figure A-13. Team process-skills scores.

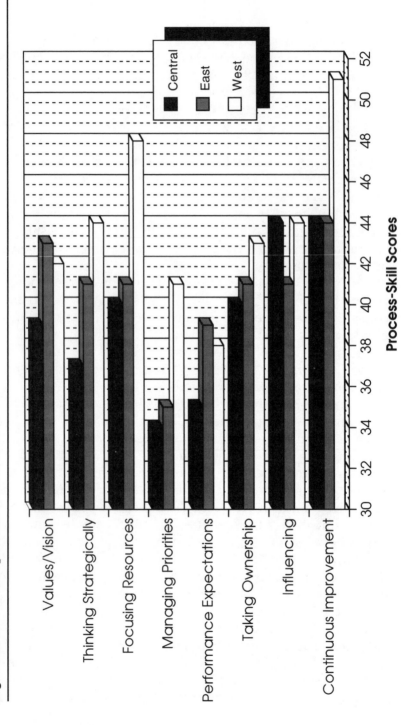

Process-Skill Scores

Figure A-14. Team knowledge quotient scores.

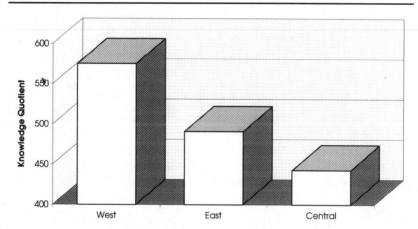

not from, its process-skill proficiency. While this objection may, in theory, seem somewhat compelling, it is not supported by the facts. In reality, the central and eastern regional teams actually received more, not less, training than their western counterpart over the five-year period. The relationship between process-skill proficiency and performance, then, is almost certainly a causal one.

Similar hypotheses were developed regarding the relative performance levels of other knowledge-work teams, all of which were equally predictive.

These results are, at the very least, highly suggestive. They lead us to confidently assert that the eight process skills measured by the P-SA are intimately and causally related to work-team performance.

Amenability of Process-Skills to Change

The final assumption underlying the use of the P-SA is that process skills and, specifically, the behaviors of which they are composed, are amenable to change. In particular, it is assumed that systematic and targeted development interventions, such as training and feedback, should affect significant process-skill and performance-quotient score improvements. Validating this inference would provide strong support for the P-SA's use as a development tool.

The measurement of change has long been a contentious issue, both conceptually and statistically, among psychometricians, with the most appropriate method still the object of heated debate. Because this dispute is yet unresolved, we have subjected the P-SA to several commonly used change measurement tests. While each test has its minor limitations, together they should provide an accurate estimate of process-skill and performance changes.

One thing on which all psychometricians agree in regard to the measurement of change is the importance of control groups. Without a control group (an assemblage of people exposed to the same conditions as the test group except in respect to the specific factor under examination) for comparison purposes, it is impossible to pinpoint the source or cause of any observed change with absolute confidence. Any score variations may result from a stimulus occurring within the boundaries of the test or from some factor outside the scope of the test system altogether. A control group, then, allows test conductors to isolate the effects of the specific variable in question.

In order to test the amenability of P-SA scores to change, the instrument was administered to a diverse sample test group of 102 knowledge workers, both before and after skills training sessions. The participants, who represented three countries, seven industries, and a wide range of income and age groups, completed the P-SA, received their feedback results and underwent Priority Management or Atheneum Learning Corporation process-skills training, and then completed a second P-SA two weeks to four months later. At no time was the test group given access, either directly or indirectly, to the P-SA Effectiveness Questionnaire answer key.

For comparative purposes, a heterogeneous sample of thirty workers followed the same basic procedure, but did not receive their P-SA feedback results or undergo training in the interim period. This sample of knowledge workers made up the control group.

The authors of the report hypothesized that those individuals who underwent training should experience substantial process-skill score increases relative to their counterparts in the control group. Several statistical techniques were employed to test this hypothesis. The first of these measured the average correlation between pre- and post-P-SA scores. The results of this test are presented in Figure A-15. The graph compares the statistical correlation among pre- and post-P-SA scores from the

Figure A-15. Correlation between pre- and post-P-SAs.

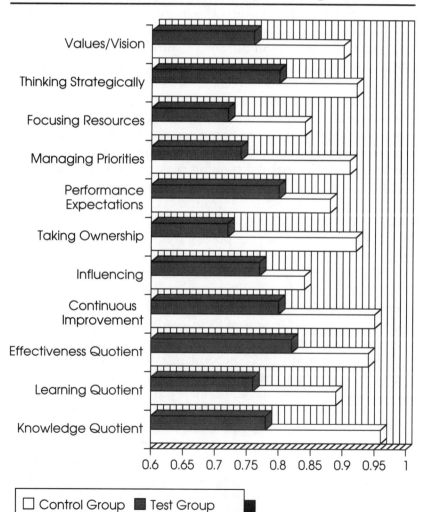

□ Control Group ■ Test Group

test group to the correlation among those from the control group. The members of the test group (that is, those individuals who underwent training after completing their first P-SAs) provided a greater range of responses on the second administration of the P-SA than on the first relative to their control group counterparts.

As expected, the average correlation is significantly weaker among pre- and post-scores from the test group than among those from the control group. The individuals who underwent training, then, provided a greater diversity of responses from one trial to the next than did their control group counterparts. Their skills-training presumably induced behavioral modifications, which translated into changes in P-SA responses on the post-training administration of the questionnaire.

While the correlation study in Figure A-15 strongly suggests that P-SA scores are amenable to systematic change, it offers no information about the direction of that change. Is it possible, though, that the training sessions actually induced a regression to lower skill levels? Although this seems ludicrous from an intuitive standpoint, from a statistical perspective it is certainly possible.

In order to test for this possibility, a second psychometric study was performed, this time measuring the average percent raw gain/loss in P-SA scores as a result of training. The results of this test are shown in Figure A-16. The graph displays the average percentage raw gain in process-skill and performance quotient scores as a result of P-SA feedback and process-skills training. The improvements vary in magnitude from 4 percent (Taking Ownership) to 27 percent (Managing Priorities), suggesting that P-SA scores are highly amenable to change.

The P-SA scores of the test group rose dramatically in every process-skill and quotient area relative to those of the control group. The score gains ranged in value from 4 percent for Taking Ownership to an astounding 27 percent for Managing Priorities. Of particular importance is the 19 percent gain in test group knowledge-quotient scores, the ultimate indicators of knowledge-worker performance. All of these increases are in direct comparison to the virtually negligible changes in control-group scores.

Figure A-16. Average precentage raw gain.

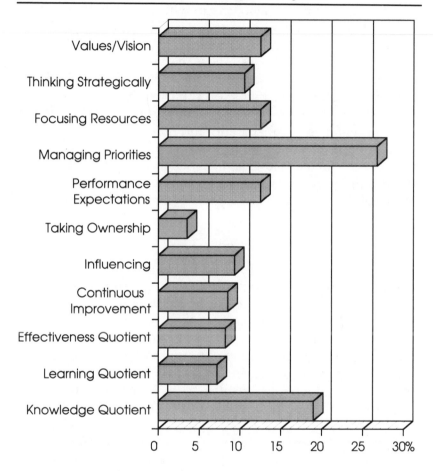

The implications of the two latter tests are unmistakable. P-SA results feedback coupled with general skills training, particularly that of Priority Management Systems and Atheneum Learning Corporation, generate dramatic P-SA score increases and, by extension, improvements in overall effectiveness.

P-SA scores are, then, highly amenable to systematic change.

One final note on validity: Most competitor diagnostic questionnaire items are actually statements (i.e., "The individual works toward the best solution in disagreements rather than trying to win") in response to which the person is scored on a Likert-type scale (usually of 1 to 5). The problem with such a rating system is that it is extremely subjective, and as such, highly prone to inaccuracies. These inaccuracies tend to reduce the validity of the corresponding instrument. The P-SA Effectiveness Questionnaire items, on the other hand, ask an individual to choose among three concrete behaviors. As a result, the P-SA is far less transparent, and so significantly more accurate than its competitors. In particular, the P-SA's scores are more closely linked to overall knowledge worker performance, and the instrument itself is better able to capture changes in skill level, two fundamental aspects of instrument validity.

Face Validity

While face validity is not typically considered in formal psychometric studies, it nonetheless does merit some attention. The effectiveness of the P-SA (and for that matter, of any psychometric instrument) hinges to a large extent on its perceived accuracy. If knowledge workers to not accept, cannot understand, question the importance of, or, for any other reason, do not buy in to their P-SA results, then the chances that these results will stimulate and guide future development decrease substantially.

In order to confirm the face validity of the P-SA, a survey was conducted with a sample of 107 knowledge workers on three continents and in multiple industries. Of the survey respondents, each of whom had completed a P-SA Effectiveness Questionnaire and subsequently reviewed his or her feedback, 95 percent either agreed or strongly agreed that each of the eight knowledge-work processes was fundamentally important to their work. In fact, less than one percent of all respondents strongly disagreed that the eight processes were integral to their work. Clearly, the P-SA feedback is widely considered both valuable and relevant.

In addition, of the same respondents, 91 percent agreed that the P-SA, on average, accurately reflected their current abilities in the eight knowledge work processes. Given that the P-SA measures effectiveness—an extremely sensitive issue for knowledge workers—these survey results are overwhelmingly positive.

Presentation of P-SA Feedback

P-SA questionnaire respondents receive a twelve-page Effectiveness Profile outlining their results. The profile, which combines both highly customized text and informative, easy-to-understand graphics, consists of six major sections.

Individual Profile

The first section of the Effectiveness Profile summarizes the respondent's process-skill results (see Figure A-17). Two columns on the left-hand side of the page outline the respondent's individual and organizational raw scores out of 60 in the eight process-skill areas. These raw scores fall in one of five development bands: Alpha, Beta, Gamma, Delta, or Epsilon. Each band represents a slice of the total population of knowledge workers who have completed the P-SA. By definition, the top 10 percent of knowledge workers and organizations score in the Alpha band, the next 20 percent fall in the Beta band, the middle 40 percent rank in the Gamma band, the next 20 percent lie in the Delta band, and the remaining 10 percent reside in the Epsilon band. The norm raw score for all knowledge workers in each process skill falls midway through the Gamma band.

The right-hand side of the page consists of two circumplexes, one individual and one organizational. Both circumplexes consist of eight process-skill quadrants, each of which is sub-divided into the five developmental bands. The quadrants are shaded to reflect the given individual's or organization's level of development in each of the process-skill areas. The upper circumplex provides a graphic profile of the individual's process-skill strengths and weaknesses relative to those of knowledge workers around the world. The lower circumplex profiles the given individual's perception of the process-skill

Figure A-17. Process-skill scores.

	PERSONAL	ORGANIZATION
kP1	42	60
kP2	50	50
kP3	51	51
kP4	42	50
kP5	32	45
kP6	31	45
kP7	60	50
kP8	41	45

PERSONAL

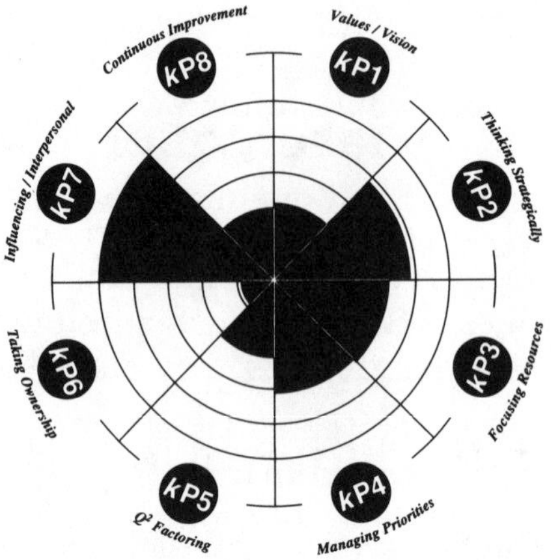

DEVELOPMENTAL BANDS

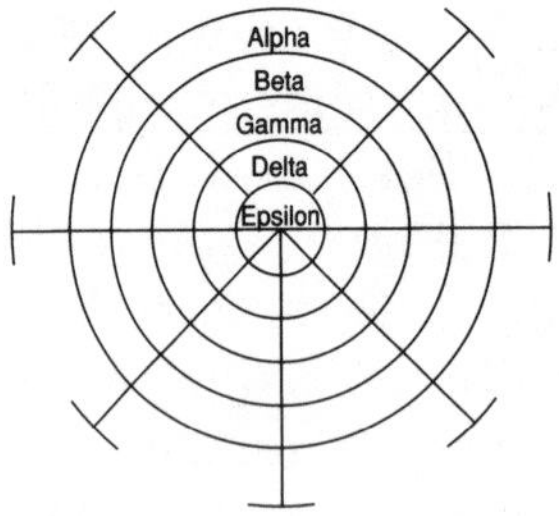

Alpha
Beta
Gamma
Delta
Epsilon

ORGANIZATION

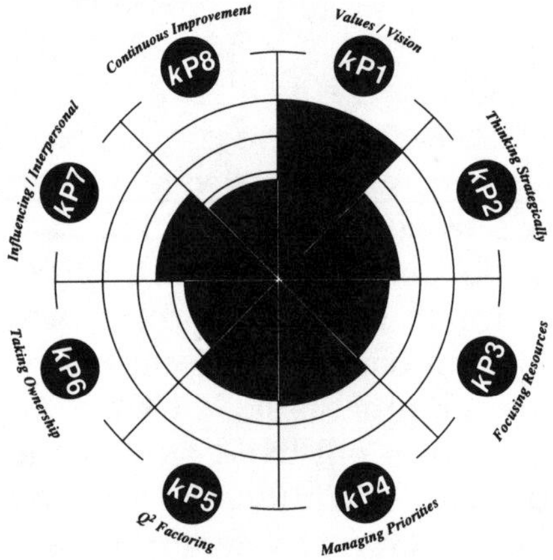

strengths and weaknesses of the organization in which he or she works relative to the perceptions of other knowledge workers in organizations around the world. Respondents can, therefore, compare their own process skills and those of their organizations to the process skills of the thousands of knowledge workers who comprise the P-SA international database. For example, an individual who receives a raw score of 57 in the area of continuous improvement falls in the Alpha band, and, therefore, is at a higher level of development in this process-skill area than at least 90 percent of all knowledge workers.

Pages three through six, which make up the second section of the report, provide detailed narrative descriptions of each process skill, as well as score-specific explanations of both individual and organizational results. A sample individual process-skill (Influencing/Interpersonal) score explanation is as follows:

> Your numerical value is 60, which is in the developmental band Alpha. Our international research has established that only 10 percent of knowledge workers achieve this top developmental band. Congratulations! This suggests that you are a highly skilled influencer who has acquired the knack for winning commitment and achieving consensus. As a consequence, you are likely to be good at taking people along with you, rather than pounding them into submission or reluctant acquiescence.

A sample organizational process-skill (Continuous Improvement) score description is as follows:

> You have placed the numerical value of your organization at 45, which is in the developmental band Gamma. You are in the same developmental band as the majority of knowledge workers. The mid-point is 41. This indicates that you perceive your part of the organization to be moderately good at actively encouraging continuous improvement practices and learning behavior. However, it is likely that there are plenty of occasions when the fundamental process of continuous improvement lapses, and the learning "habit" is temporarily abandoned. Continuous improvement is exactly that—continuous. It isn't a process that comes and goes or is ever completed.

The next major section (see Figure A-18) contains three sets of bar graphs, each representing a separate performance quotient derived from the raw process-skill scores. The first of these is the Effectiveness Quotient (EQ), which, rated on a scale of 1–100, is an indicator of overall effectiveness based on the average of the ratings achieved in all eight key processes. The second

Figure A-18. Performance quotients.

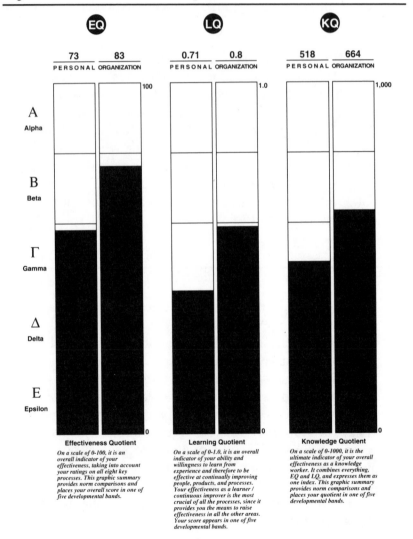

key performance index is the Learning Quotient (LQ). On a scale of 0–1.0, it is a measure of willingness and ability to learn from experience, and therefore to be effective at continually improving people, products, and processes. Learning/Continuous Improvement is the most crucial of all work processes, since it unlocks the door to future success. The final indicator, the Knowledge Quotient (KQ), combines both the Effectiveness and Learning Quotients to establish an overall performance index. On a scale of 0–1000, it is a measure of current effectiveness (EQ) coupled with the ability and desire to learn (LQ), and thus probability of future effectiveness. The Knowledge Quotient is the most important indicator of "white collar" performance.

The performance-quotient section presents both individual and organizational bar graphs, each of which is sub-divided into five developmental bands. This allows individuals to compare their performance levels and those of their organizations to those of individuals and organizations around the world.

It is absolutely essential to remember that the above performance quotients are not static indexes. They are simply accurate "snapshots" of effectiveness, and, like the process-skills scores from which they are derived, can be improved with the appropriate feedback and training interventions.

Pages eight and nine provide detailed score-dependent narrative explanations of the individual and organizational performance quotient scores. A sample individual quotient (Knowledge) explanation is as follows:

> Your numerical value is 518, which is in the developmental band Gamma. You are in the moderate band as an effective knowledge worker. The mid-point for knowledge workers is 527, so 50 percent of knowledge workers place higher than this. Your Knowledge Quotient is the ultimate indicator of your overall effectiveness as a knowledge worker. It combines your Effectiveness Quotient and your Learning Quotient, and expresses them as one index. This suggests there are some areas for improvement before you are functioning as a fully effective knowledge worker.

A sample organizational quotient (Effectiveness) score description is as follows:

> You have placed the numerical value of your organization at 83, which is in the developmental band Beta. You are in the high band, which indicates that you perceive your organization to have high overall effectiveness. Only 10 percent of knowledge workers place in a higher band. The Effectiveness Quotient is an overall indicator of the way you see the effectiveness of your organization based on all eight key processes. Your result shows that you feel your organization enjoys a high level of effectiveness across the eight key processes.

The next, and perhaps most revealing components of the P-SA Effectiveness Profile are the individual and organizational Effectiveness Gap Analyses. The Personal Gap Analysis (see Figure A-19) benchmarks the individual process-skill and quotient scores against those of the ideal knowledge worker and the international average knowledge worker. An individual can also compare himself or herself to a series of more specific norms, such as industry, age group, income bracket, organizational, department, and team averages.

To the right of each process skill and quotient on the Personal Gap Analysis page is a scale of 0–100, on which several symbols appear. The symbol "$_\square$" denotes the individual score on the given process skill or quotient, while the character "•" represents the international score in each of the same areas. The first column of numbers to the right of the scale represents the difference between the given individual's score and that of the hypothetical ideal knowledge worker. Zero, then, is the optimum score, with negative values indicating lesser degrees of competency. A value of -33, for example, means that the individual is 33 increments less competent in the given area than is the perfect worker. The second column of numbers compares the individual's score to that of the international average knowledge worker. In this case, zero is an average score, negative values represent greater developmental opportunities,

Figure A-19. Personal gap analysis.

PROCESS · SKILL	0 10 20 30 40 50 60 70 80 90 100	GAP ANALYSIS Ideal	International Average		
(kP1) Values / Vision	□ ● (at ~70)	−30	−7		
(kP2) Thinking Strategically	● (at ~60) □ (at ~75)	−17	15		
(kP3) Focusing Resources	● (at ~65) □ (at ~80)	−15	10		
(kP4) Managing Priorities	●□ (at ~65)	−30	3		
(kP5) Q² Factoring	□● (at ~50)	−47	−5		
(kP6) Taking Ownership	□ (at ~55) ● (at ~70)	−48	−23		
(kP7) Influencing / Interpersonal	● (at ~70) □ (at ~85)	0	25		
(kP8) Continuous Improvement	□ ● (at ~65)	−32	−8		

	0 10 20 30 40 50 60 70 80 90 100				
(EQ) Effectiveness Quotient	●□ (at ~65)	−27	3		

	0.0 0.1 0.2 0.3 0.4 0.5 0.6 0.7 0.8 0.9 1.0				
(LQ) Learning Quotient	□ ● (at ~0.75)	−0.29	−0.05		

	0 200 400 600 800 1000				
(KQ) Knowledge Quotient	●□ (at ~450)	−482	−9		

K
E   □ Personal
Y   ● International Average of Individual Profiles

and positive scores symbolize higher levels of proficiency. A value of 14, for example, means that the individual is 14 increments more competent in the given area than is the average knowledge worker.

The Organization Gap Analysis (see Figure A-20) employs an identical format to benchmark the organization's process-

Figure A-20. Organization gap analysis.

PROCESS · SKILL	Ideal	International Average
kP1 Values / Vision	0	25
kP2 Thinking Strategically	−17	17
kP3 Focusing Resources	−15	10
kP4 Managing Priorities	−17	17
kP5 Q^2 Factoring	−25	13
kP6 Taking Ownership	−25	−2
kP7 Influencing / Interpersonal	−17	17
kP8 Continuous Improvement	−25	7
EQ Effectiveness Quotient	−17	15
LQ Learning Quotient	−0.2	0.09
KQ Knowledge Quotient	−336	188

K
E   ☐ Perception of Organization/Team
Y   ● International Average of Perception of Organization/Team Profiles

skill and quotient scores against those of the ideal organization and the average international company.

The final section of the P-SA Effectiveness Profile outlines certain key criteria that should guide construction of a development plan based on the results of the P-SA. The plan should be specific (detailing who will do what, when, and where), feasible (realistic), selective (focusing on areas of greatest opportunity), and immediate (concentrating on things you can implement quickly).

Colleague Perception Profile

A Colleague Perception Profile provides a knowledge worker with 360-degree feedback—that is, input from colleagues at multiple organizational levels, at least one of which is from above (e.g., a supervisor), one from below (e.g., a direct report), and one from the same level (e.g., a peer) as the individual being assessed.

The report follows the same basic format as the individual feedback profile with only a few minor differences. In addition to the standard individual and organizational data and features, the colleague profile contains raw process-skill scores, a circumplex, score-dependent narratives, knowledge quotients, and a gap analysis based on the combined feedback of at least three fellow employees. An individual can, therefore, directly compare his or her process-skill self-perception to the average perception of multiple observers.

The Colleague Perception Profile, then, is a powerful tool that offers respondents a 360-degree portrait of their overall effectiveness.

Executive Profile

A group or "Executive" P-SA Effectiveness Profile also employs the same format as the individual feedback report. It highlights the process-skill strengths and weaknesses of work teams and their organizations as the teams perceive them.

Raw team scores are based on the average of all members in the given group and are compared to those of the knowledge work teams that make up the P-SA international database.

The Executive P-SA Effectiveness Profile Gap Analyses allow a team to compare its process-skill and quotient scores to those of the ideal knowledge work team and the international average team. It also offers the option of comparing the given team scores to those of other teams within the same organization and industry.

The Executive Profile, then, enables teams to identify their process-skill strengths and weaknesses, and focus resources in areas of greatest developmental need.

Supplemental Tables

Finally, we are providing you with three tables to supplement this Appendix.

Figures A-21 and A-22 provide additional statistical information on the P-SA process skills and behavioral items we've discussed. The table in Figure A-21 outlines the standard deviation scores for each individual and process-skill area. The chart in Figure A-22 details the average scores on the ninety-six P-SA behavioral items. (Remember: The P-SA Effectiveness Questionnaire comprises ninety-six behaviorally based multiple choice questions.)

The table in Figure A-23 compares the average raw percentage change in P-SA scores of the test group (the 102 knowledge workers who completed P-SAs both before and after training) relative to the change in control group (the thirty knowledge workers who completed P-SAs, but with no intermittent training) scores.

Figure A-21. Process-skill score standard deviation.

	Individual SD	Organizational SD
Values/Vision	8.5	11.3
Thinking Strategically	9.5	13.6
Focusing Resources	8.5	10.5
Managing Priorities	9.7	11.9
Performance Expectations	8.3	11.1
Taking Ownership	6.5	10.7
Influencing	9.1	12.1
Continuous Improvement	8.4	14.3

Figure A-22. Average item scores.

ITEM #	AVERAGE	ITEM #	AVERAGE
1	8.8	49	8.6
2	8.7	50	7.6
3	7.3	51	6.7
4	5.1	52	4.7
5	7.1	53	5.9
6	6.8	54	7.5
7	7.3	55	6.7
8	8.9	56	7.7
9	5.9	57	6.8
10	4.9	58	6.1
11	4.7	59	5.7
12	3.6	60	4.2
13	5.9	61	7.3
14	7.5	62	7.6
15	5.6	63	6.3
16	5.9	64	6.4
17	7.5	65	6.8
18	6.1	66	6.4
19	5.9	67	6.6
20	7.8	68	6.6
21	5.3	69	5.8
22	9.5	70	8.4
23	8.6	71	6.8
24	8.1	72	6.7
25	7.3	73	6.7
26	7	74	5.8
27	9.1	75	7.6
28	6.1	76	6
29	5.3	77	5.9
30	7.7	78	7
31	5	79	4.5
32	7.5	80	6.9
33	7.2	81	7.2
34	7.3	82	6.6
35	8.3	83	7.7
36	5.9	84	6.2
37	5.5	85	5.3
38	5.9	86	6
39	7.3	87	7.2
40	5.2	88	5.9
41	7.3	89	6.5
42	5.1	90	5
43	7.3	91	7.6
44	7.3	92	7.9
45	6.1	93	5.4
46	5.7	94	6.6
47	8.6	95	8
48	9.6	96	7.6

Figure A-23. Average percentage raw change.

	Test Group	Control Group
Values/Vision	12.10%	-1.10%
Thinking Strategically	10.30%	3.70%
Focusing Resources	12.90%	-0.36%
Managing Priorities	26.60%	-1.80%
Performance Expectations	12.70%	-1.80%
Taking Ownership	3.60%	1.70%
Influencing	9.60%	1.70%
Continuous Improvement	9%	1.10%
Effectiveness Quotient	8.60%	0.16%
Learning Quotient	7.80%	2.60%
Knowledge Quotient	18.70%	3%

Conclusion

The Process-Skills Analysis, a theoretically sound, well-developed, highly reliable, and rigorously validated tool, enables individuals, teams, or entire organizations to compare their effectiveness in each of the eight process skills against actual benchmarks established from a database of thousands of participants around the world. Furthermore, the results of the analysis provide a graphic representation pinpointing areas with the greatest need for improvement. This accurate analysis tool, then, allows you to focus both personal and organizational skill-development and chart a path to enhanced effectiveness.

Knowledge workers in the 1990s—now, the overwhelming majority of the workforce of industrialized nations—face the effectiveness challenge of improved productivity, quality, and interdependence. Priority Management/Atheneum has cracked the "effectiveness code." Our Process-Skills Analysis will help you and your organization make significant improvements in the vital skill areas and, in turn, your long-term success and profitability. It is the key to success in the New Economy.

Glossary

behavioral item A word, phrase, sentence, or question that relates to some aspect of behavior.

cluster analysis A statistical technique that groups like objects or items.

construct An abstract variable that cannot be directly measured.

core competency An indicator of the skill and ability to effectively perform a knowledge-work process.

correlation A numeric indication of the strength of the relationship between two variables.

effectiveness quotient An indicator of current effectiveness based on the average of the ratings achieved on the eight fundamental process skills.

face validity The degree to which an instrument's scores appear on the surface to be accurate.

internal consistency The average correlation among items making up a scale.

item A word, phrase, sentence, or question that describes an aspect of behavior, performance, skill, or personality.

knowledge quotient An index of current effectiveness coupled with the ability and willingness to learn and, thus, probability of future effectiveness. The knowledge quotient is the most important measure of knowledge-worker performance.

learning quotient A measure of willingness and ability to learn from experience and, therefore, to be effective at continually improving people, products, and processes.

norms The average scores of all people who have taken the instrument or the average scores of specific target groups.

psychometric instrument A tool that numerically estimates aspects of performance or behavior.

reliability The degree to which a psychometric instrument is free from unsystematic errors of measurement.

sample A subset of individuals drawn from the total population or database.

scale A group of items that have theoretical and empirical coherence.

standard deviation A measurement of the amount of spread in the distribution of scores about the average.

test-retest reliability Stability of instrument scores over short periods of time.

validation The process of accumulating support for the inferences underlying the uses of a psychometric instrument.

validity The degree to which inferences made from an instrument's scores are legitimate, useful, and meaningful.

References

American Psychological Association. *Standards for Educational and Psychological Testing*. Washington, D.C.: American Psychological Association, 1985.

Bell, D. *The Coming of Post-Industrial Society*. New York: Basic Books, 1983.

Blackburn, P., R. Coombs, and K. Green. *Technology, Economic Growth, and the Labor Process*. New York: St. Martin's Press, 1985.

Carnevale, Anthony P. *America and the New Economy*. Alexandria, Virginia: American Society for Training and Development, 1991.

Carnevale, Anthony P. and L. Gainer. *The Learning Enterprise*. Washington, D.C.: U.S. Department of Labor and American Society for Training and Development, 1989.

Clark, K. E. and M. B. Clark (editors). *Measures of Leadership*. West Orange, New Jersey: Leadership Library of America, 1990.

Cronbach, L. J. and L. Furby. "How Should We Measure 'Change'— Or Should We?" *Psychological Bulletin* (1970), vol. 74, no. 1, pp. 68–80.

Cronbach, L. J. and Goldine C. Gleser. *Psychological Tests and Personnel Decisions*. Urbana: University of Illinois Press, 1965.

Edwards, R. *Contested Terrain: The Transformation of the Workplace in the Twentieth Century*. New York: Basic Books, 1979.

Garside, R. F. "The Regression of Gains Upon Initial Scores." *Psychometrika* (1956), vol. 21, pp. 67–77.

Gerber, Sterling K. and Nancy A. Gulanick. "Internal Invalidity in Pretest–Posttest Self-Report Evaluations and a Re-Evaluation of Retrospective Pretests." *Applied Psychological Measurement* (1979), vol. 3, no. 1, pp. 1–23.

Golembiewski, R. T. "The Alpha, Beta, Gamma Change Typology: Perspectives on Acceptance as Well as Resistance." *Group and Organizational Studies* (1989), vol. 14, no. 2, pp. 150–154.

Golembiewski, R. T. and Carl W. Proehl. "Estimating the Success of

OD Applications." *Training and Development Journal* (1982), vol. 36, no. 4, pp. 86–95.

Grayson, C. and C. O'Dell. *American Business: A Two-Minute Warning.* New York: The Free Press, 1988.

Guilford, J. P. *Psychometric Models.* New York: McGraw-Hill, 1954.

Helmstadter, G. C. *Principles of Psychological Measurement.* New York: Meredith Publishing Company.

Johnston, W. and A. Packer. *Work Force 2000: Work and Workers for the 21st Century.* Indianapolis: Hudson Institute, 1987.

Keyser, D. J. and R. Sweetland (editors). *Tests: A Comprehensive Reference for Assessment in Psychology, Education, and Business* (2nd edition). Austin, Texas: Pro-ed, 1986.

Kouzes, James M. and Barry Z. Posner. "Development and Validation of the Leadership Practices Inventory." *Educational and Psychological Measurement* (1988), vol. 48, pp. 483–496.

Leslie, Jean Brittain, and Ellen Van Velsor. *Feedback to Managers, Volume I: A Review and Comparison of Sixteen Multi-Rater Feedback Instruments.* Greensboro, North Carolina: Center for Creative Leadership, 1991.

Leslie, Jean Brittain, and Ellen Van Velsor. *Feedback to Managers, Volume II: A Guide to Evaluating Multi-Rater Feedback Instruments.* Greensboro, North Carolina: Center for Creative Leadership, 1991.

Lord, F. M. "Further Problems in the Measurement of Growth." *Educational Psychological Measurement* (1958), vol. 18, pp. 437–454.

Mitchell, J. (editor). *Mental Measurements Yearbook: the Buros Institute of Mental Measurements* (9th edition). Lincoln, Nebraska: The University of Nebraska, 1985.

Nunnally, Jum C. *Psychometric Theory.* New York: McGraw-Hill, 1967.

Weitzman, R. A. "Test-Retest Reliability of Formula Scored Multiple Choice Test." *Psychological Reports* (1984), pp. 419–425.

Windle, C. "Test-Retest Effect on Personality Questionnaires." *Educational Psychological Measurement* (1954), vol. 14, pp. 617–633.

Index